Sugar Reef
CARIBBEAN COOKING

QUANTITY SALES

Most Dell books are available at special quantity discounts when purchased in bulk by corporations, organizations, and special-interest groups. Custom imprinting or excerpting can also be done to fit special needs. For details write: Dell Publishing, 666 Fifth Avenue, New York, NY 10103. Attn.: Special Sales Department.

INDIVIDUAL SALES

Are there any Dell books you want but cannot find in your local stores? If so, you can order them directly from us. You can get any Dell book in print. Simply include the book's title, author, and ISBN number if you have it, along with a check or money order (no cash can be accepted) for the full retail price plus $2.00 to cover shipping and handling. Mail to: Dell Readers Service, P.O. Box 5057, Des Plaines, IL 60017.

SUGAR REEF

Caribbean Cooking

DEVRA DEDEAUX

A Dell Trade Paperback

A DELL TRADE PAPERBACK
Published by
Dell Publishing
a division of
Bantam Doubleday Dell Publishing Group, Inc.
666 Fifth Avenue
New York, New York 10103

ISBN: 0-440-50336-1

Reprinted by arrangement with McGraw-Hill Book Company

Printed in the United States of America

Published simultaneously in Canada.

March 1991

10 9 8 7 6 5 4 3 2 1

RRH

This book is dedicated to the memory of
William "Zami" Zamora
and to all the willing guinea pigs
who suffered and savored the testing
of these recipes.

CONTENTS

Appetizers & Salads

Soups

Seafood

INTRODUCTION

*T*rue Caribbean food can be found in the many small Creole kitchens nestled along the shores of the islands, where native cooks prepare simple and hearty fare that reflects a blending of cultures unique to each place. Among those who contributed to the mix are the original inhabitants of the islands, the Carib and Arawak Indians, as well as the Africans, East Indians, and Chinese who were forced to the West Indies in slavery. Add some British, French, Spanish, and Dutch settlers to the pot, and the results are a wondrous combining and recombining of foods, techniques, and ideas.

The native inhabitants of the Caribbean were quickly wiped out. If they did not perish at the hands of their European conquerors, the Indians committed suicide, which they preferred to slavery. Although they had taught early settlers about the foods of their islands, it was predominantly African slaves who established the foundation of Caribbean cuisine. To the Africans the survival of their culture was of the utmost importance but was nearly impossible under the harsh reality of slavery. The foods they ate and the religions they practiced were all they had to cling to, apart from their precious memories. Food helped to ensure the continued existence of their culture, and they smuggled cargos of peas, okra, and yams onto slave ships, then cultivated them in foreign soil to help them adjust to their new home. These ingredients laid the course of Caribbean cuisine.

What is so remarkable about the West Indies is the variety of tastes and techniques that makes each island's food distinctive. The entire region has strong ties to African cooking, but there are other influences also at work. The stronger the dominance a European empire had upon an island, the stronger the influence that culture had upon its food. In places like the Dominican Republic and Puerto Rico, cooking has a definite Spanish character, as demonstrated by the presence of such ingredients as olives, capers, garlic, and coriander (*cilantro*). On Guadeloupe and Martinique the use of fresh herbs and cream-based sauces marks the heavy influence of the French upon their cuisine. On islands once ruled by the British, like Jamaica, the natives stop for afternoon tea and enjoy dinners of curried meats with homemade chutney. Their rum cakes are delicious and could pass for any English Christmas pudding in a blindfold test. Then there are the Dutch islands like Curaçao, where the people speak a language that blends African, Spanish, French, Dutch, and Portuguese. The national dish is a meat-filled Edam cheese—only the Dutch could think of that.

Food plays a central role in family life and

traditions in this part of the world, and cooks spend days preparing foods for holidays, festivals, and special family gatherings. Such an emphasis on family means that native Caribbeans rarely eat out. As a result, on many of the islands it can be very difficult for nonnatives to find authentic Caribbean cuisine. Most restaurants cater to the taste of American tourists, so visitors must seek out those that serve the foods of the people.

One such restaurant exists on an island, but it is far to the north of the Caribbean Sea. Sugar Reef is the youngest sibling of two other Manhattan eateries—Tortilla Flats, serving Tex-Mex cuisine, and Gulf Coast, featuring the foods of the southern Gulf Coast states. These cuisines proved to be extremely popular with New York diners, and the restaurants prospered. So much so that the original owners, Sherry Delamarter, Jay Savulich, and Barry Secular, decided to add two new partners to their group, Zeet Peabody and Devra Dedeaux, and formulate plans for a third venture.

Caribbean food seemed the logical choice, given the public's enthusiasm for hot and hotter foods. The progression was natural for us for several reasons. The kitchen staffs at both Tortilla Flats and Gulf Coast were natives of either the Dominican Republic or Puerto Rico. Every day they would prepare for themselves spicy Caribbean lunches of fried *chicarrones*, sweet plantains, and beans and rice. Secondly, the partners had collectively gathered a wealth of ideas and inspiration from extensive travels to the islands. We had been welcomed into Caribbean homes and shared in family customs and wonderful food.

Each year we return to the Caribbean in search of new friends and good food and to plan the future of the restaurant. We bring back recipes and adapt them to our kitchen, which keeps our menu fresh and exciting as well as authentic. Each year we also invite a well-known cook from the islands to be guest chef at Sugar Reef for a week. Not only does this serve as a great cultural exchange, but it allows us to highlight one island for the week and to enlighten our customers about its customs and cuisine.

Sugar Reef Caribbean Cooking was a natural outgrowth of this successful venture. In it we present a diverse sampling of the recipes we have gathered from throughout the Caribbean, as well as some inventions of our brilliant chef, Pablo Rosado, who is a native of the Dominican Republic. All are characteristic of the islands, and all have met the ultimate test—approval by our customers. We think you'll like them too. So mix yourself a Goombay Smash, heat up the grill, and enjoy!

CARIBBEAN INGREDIENTS

*T*he ingredients used in Caribbean cooking do not vary much from island to island. Tropical fruits and vegetables are abundant everywhere, as well as a vast array of seafoods, and the islands share similar climates and terrain. What makes the food of the islands different is the way West Indian cooks combine these ingredients.

We urge you to do as the natives do—use only the freshest and best ingredients available. Use only fresh lemon and lime juice, fruits and vegetables, and the freshest possible fish, poultry, and meat. The recipes in this book indicate when a substitute is admissible. Otherwise, if you can't find an ingredient, try another recipe before trying a substitute.

Throughout the book and in the glossary, you'll find information about many of the ingredients used in Caribbean cooking. If you are puzzled about an unfamiliar one, the index will tell you where it is described. Some ingredients require special handling or techniques, which are described below.

Hot Peppers
Peppers came to the Caribbean from Africa, where the climate and vegetation are similar to what is found on the islands. Before refrigeration peppers served as preservatives because they are good at controlling and killing bacteria in food. Today they are made into hot sauces mixed with vinegar, mustard, onions, green papayas, and herbs.

For most of the recipes in this book we specify the Scotch bonnet pepper, which is the most widely used in the islands. It is shaped much like a Scotsman's bonnet, and the pods range from red to orange to yellow and green. You may substitute jalapeño, serrano, or the hottest fresh pepper available.

Hot peppers require careful handling and can burn the skin and irritate the eyes. You must wash your hands after chopping these little monsters. If you have sensitive skin, coat your hands with vegetable oil or wear plastic or rubber gloves.

Coconut Cream
Also known as coconut milk, this ingredient should not be confused with the liquid found in the center of a coconut when it is cracked open. The cream is obtained by grating the meat of a ripe coconut, covering it with a cup of hot water, and squeezing it through a piece of muslin or cheesecloth to extract a thick, creamy liquid. If you can find commercially prepared coconut cream, buy it. It is just as good as homemade and will save you a lot of work. (Be sure to get the unsweetened kind unless you are making piña coladas.)

Pineapple
When choosing a fresh pineapple, test it for ripeness by pulling a leaf from the center of the crown. If the leaf pulls out easily, the fruit is ripe and ready. To cut open a pineapple, lay it on its side and slice it in half lengthwise. You will see a woody core running the length of the fruit and surrounded by juice meat. Cut out the core, which is not edible, and slice the remaining meat or quarter the sections. Cut away the prickly outer skin and eat.

Here is a pineapple fact: Raw pineapples contain an enzyme called bromeline, which aids the body in the digestion of food. Cooking the pineapple zaps the enzyme of its power. This means that fresh pineapple at the end of a meal is not only delicious but smart.

Plantains
Unlike the banana, which it resembles, the plantain has a skin that is somewhat difficult to remove without a trick or two. We find it best to slice off both ends of the plantain and cut it in half lengthwise. Then cut four evenly spaced lengthwise slits in the skin of each half, being careful not to cut through to the flesh. Next, beginning at the tip of the plantain, slowly peel away each strip of skin. For best results, pull the skin off crosswise, not parallel, to the fruit.

Curry

Curry was incorporated into Caribbean cuisine by the East Indians who were brought to the British colonies to work the fields as slaves along with the Africans. Curry is an important ingredient in Caribbean cooking and evolved into a variety of styles, depending upon the island. Although commercial curry powder is fine for the recipes in this book, we urge you to try one of these examples of island curry.

Jamaica

½	cup ground coriander
½	cup ground turmeric
2	tablespoons ground fenugreek
½	cup ground ginger
½	cup ground black pepper
2	tablespoons ground cardamom
2	tablespoons ground cinnamon

Trinidad/Guyana

1½	teaspoons ground cloves
1½	teaspoons ground poppyseed
1	tablespoon ground coriander
1½	teaspoons ground mustard
2	tablespoons ground cumin
1	tablespoon ground cayenne pepper
2	tablespoons ground cinnamon
1½	teaspoons ground black pepper
6	tablespoons ground turmeric
¼	cup ground ginger

French Islands

¼	teaspoon turmeric
2	teaspoons ground coriander
2	teaspoons ground mustard
2	teaspoons garlic powder
1	teaspoon saffron
1	teaspoon ground black pepper
1	teaspoon cayenne pepper
2	teaspoons tamarind pulp

Dried Salt Cod

The cod has historically been the most important fish in the world. No other fish can be salted more successfully or holds up better after curing. New England salt cod played an especially important role in the slave trade. It was bought to feed slaves on the sugar plantations of the West Indies and was paid for in molasses, which was shipped back to New England for making rum.

To prepare dried salt cod, soak it in water overnight, covered and refrigerated. Remove from the refrigerator and drain. Fill a stockpot with water, bring to a boil, and add the codfish. Boil the fish for about 10 minutes and drain. Repeat this step by filling the stockpot again and boiling the fish for another 10 minutes. Drain the fish and pat it dry with paper towels. Wrap it in a double thickness of cheesecloth and squeeze out the remaining water. Unwrap and remove any skin and bones.

Conch

The conch (pronounced conk) is best known to American tourists for its lovely conical pink shell. It's the big shell you hold up to your ear to hear the sound of the sea. But to natives of the Caribbean, the conch is prized for its tasty meat, which somewhat resembles the clam in flavor.

Fresh conch is tough and must be pounded with a meat mallet to tenderize it. Use the flat, not spiked side of the mallet and pound the meat for several minutes or until it is considerably flatter than it was originally. Avoid overcooking or the meat will become tough again. Conch is difficult to find outside Florida and the Caribbean, but you can substitute canned conch with good results, especially in chowders and fritters.

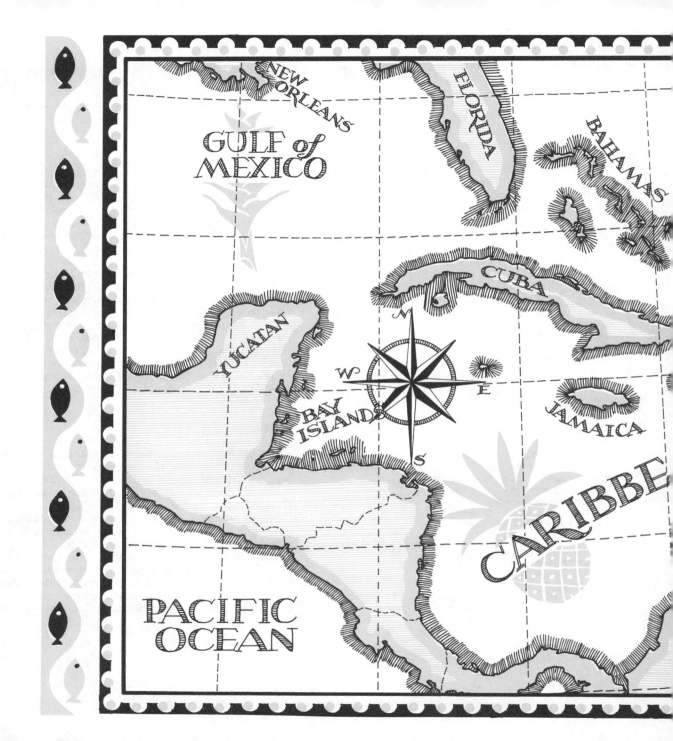

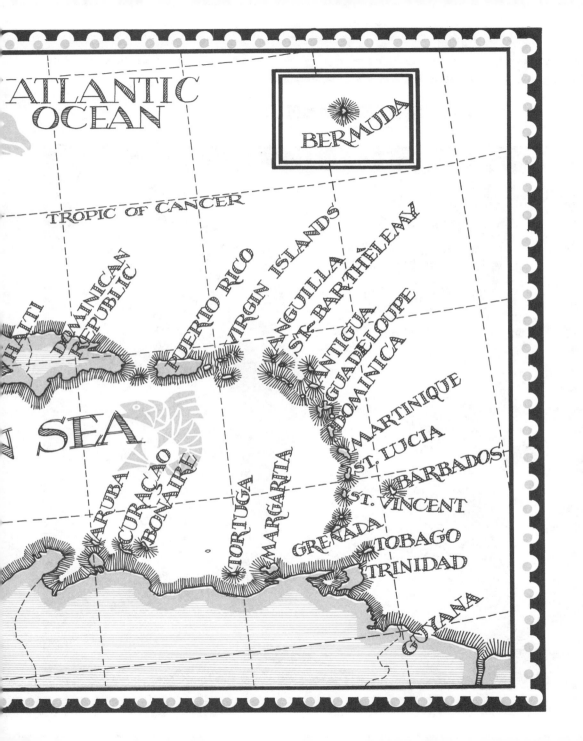

ATLANTIC
OCEAN

BERMUDA

TROPIC OF CANCER

HAITI
DOMINICAN REPUBLIC
PUERTO RICO
VIRGIN ISLANDS
ANGUILLA
ST-BARTHELEMY
ANTIGUA
GUADELOUPE
DOMINICA

N SEA

ARUBA
CURAÇAO
BONAIRE

TORTUGA
MARGARITA

MARTINIQUE
ST. LUCIA
BARBADOS
ST. VINCENT

GRENADA
TOBAGO
TRINIDAD

GUYANA

13

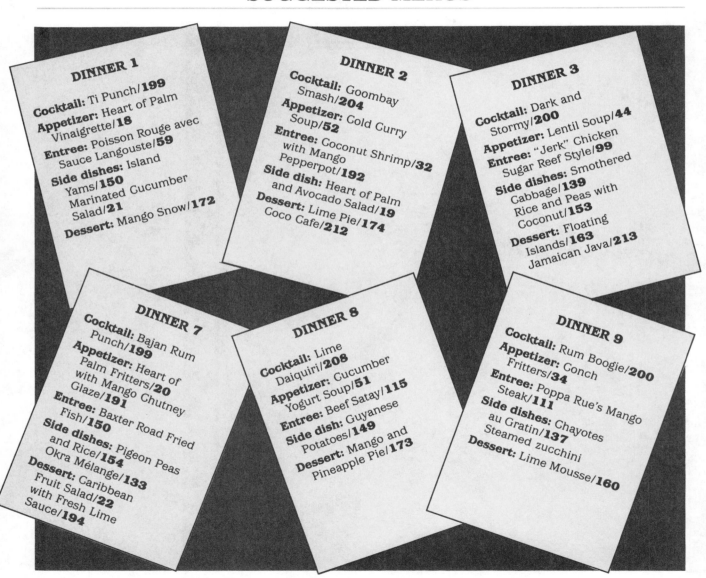

DINNER 1

Cocktail: Ti Punch/**199**
Appetizer: Heart of Palm
Vinaigrette/**18**
Entree: Poisson Rouge avec
Sauce Langouste/**59**
Side dishes: Island
Yams/**150**
Marinated Cucumber
Salad/**21**
Dessert: Mango Snow/**172**

DINNER 2

Cocktail: Goombay
Smash/**204**
Appetizer: Cold Curry
Soup/**52**
Entree: Coconut Shrimp/**32**
with Mango
Pepperpot/**192**
Side dish: Heart of Palm
and Avocado Salad/**19**
Dessert: Lime Pie/**174**
Coco Cafe/**212**

DINNER 3

Cocktail: Dark and
Stormy/**200**
Appetizer: Lentil Soup/**44**
Entree: "Jerk" Chicken
Sugar Reef Style/**99**
Side dishes: Smothered
Gabbage/**139**
Rice and Peas with
Coconut/**153**
Dessert: Floating
Islands/**163**
Jamaican Java/**213**

DINNER 7

Cocktail: Bajan Rum
Punch/**199**
Appetizer: Heart of
Palm Fritters/**20**
with Mango Chutney
Glaze/**191**
Entree: Baxter Road Fried
Fish/**150**
Side dishes: Pigeon Peas
and Rice/**154**
Okra Mélange/**133**
Dessert: Caribbean
Fruit Salad/**22**
with Fresh Lime
Sauce/**194**

DINNER 8

Cocktail: Lime
Daiquiri/**208**
Appetizer: Cucumber
Yogurt Soup/**51**
Entree: Beef Satay/**115**
Side dish: Guyanese
Potatoes/**149**
Dessert: Mango and
Pineapple Pie/**173**

DINNER 9

Cocktail: Rum Boogie/**200**
Appetizer: Conch
Fritters/**34**
Entree: Poppa Rue's Mango
Steak/**111**
Side dishes: Chayotes
au Gratin/**137**
Steamed zucchini
Dessert: Lime Mousse/**160**

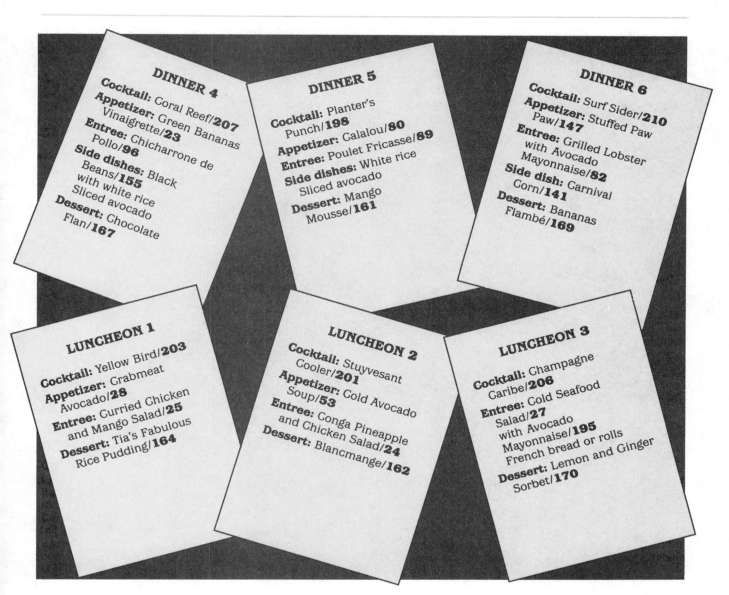

DINNER 4

Cocktail: Coral Reef/**207**
Appetizer: Green Bananas
 Vinaigrette/**23**
Entree: Chicharrone de
 Pollo/**96**
Side dishes: Black
 Beans/**155**
 with white rice
 Sliced avocado
Dessert: Chocolate
 Flan/**167**

DINNER 5

Cocktail: Planter's
 Punch/**198**
Appetizer: Galalou/**80**
Entree: Poulet Fricasse/**89**
Side dishes: White rice
 Sliced avocado
Dessert: Mango
 Mousse/**161**

DINNER 6

Cocktail: Surf Sider/**210**
Appetizer: Stuffed Paw
 Paw/**147**
Entree: Grilled Lobster
 with Avocado
 Mayonnaise/**82**
Side dish: Carnival
 Corn/**141**
Dessert: Bananas
 Flambé/**169**

LUNCHEON 1

Cocktail: Yellow Bird/**203**
Appetizer: Crabmeat
 Avocado/**28**
Entree: Curried Chicken
 and Mango Salad/**25**
Dessert: Tia's Fabulous
 Rice Pudding/**164**

LUNCHEON 2

Cocktail: Stuyvesant
 Cooler/**201**
Appetizer: Cold Avocado
 Soup/**53**
Entree: Conga Pineapple
 and Chicken Salad/**24**
Dessert: Blancmange/**162**

LUNCHEON 3

Cocktail: Champagne
 Caribe/**206**
Entree: Cold Seafood
 Salad/**27**
 with Avocado
 Mayonnaise/**195**
 French bread or rolls
Dessert: Lemon and Ginger
 Sorbet/**170**

Appetizers & Salads

HEART OF PALM VINAIGRETTE

A lot of customers ask us, "What is heart of palm?" The response is usually . . . the heart of palm. Of course, we get back perplexed looks, so we follow with another explanation: it is the delicate meat from the heart of the palm tree and tastes much like an artichoke. Although we rarely find the real thing in the United States, it is generally available canned in water. Rinse and drain and it is just fine. In this recipe, common on the French islands, the palm is thinly sliced and topped with a tasty vinaigrette.

1 14-ounce can heart of palm, rinsed and drained

Juice of 1 lime

Lettuce leaves, for garnish

Tomato wedges, for garnish

Finely chopped fresh coriander, for garnish

VINAIGRETTE:

¾ cup olive oil

¼ cup white wine vinegar

⅓ cup orange juice

2 tablespoons Dijon mustard

2 cloves garlic, minced

½ teaspoon salt

½ teaspoon freshly ground black pepper

1. Slice the heart of palm lengthwise into thin sticks (like shoestring potatoes). Place in a bowl, sprinkle with the lime juice, toss lightly, and cover. Refrigerate to chill for about 1 hour.

2. Just before you are ready to serve, prepare the vinaigrette. In a small bowl, combine the olive oil, vinegar, orange juice, mustard, garlic, salt, and pepper with a wire whisk until the ingredients are well blended.

3. Line individual salad plates with lettuce leaves. Arrange the heart of palm on top and pour on the vinaigrette. Garnish with tomato wedges and coriander.

Serves 4

Appetizers & Salads

HEART OF PALM AND AVOCADO SALAD

This salad includes two staples of the Caribbean isles—avocado and heart of palm, whose delicate flavors complement each other well. With a vinaigrette, *c'est formidable!* Easy, too.

Isla de Margarita

In Spanish this island's name means "pearl." Not many people know of Margarita, which is just 18 miles off the coast of Venezuela. At one time it was famous for the pearls found off its shores; these are rare today. Islanders in this friendly place eat large meals in the middle of the day and late dinners that include flying fish, lobster, red snapper, mangoes, pineapple, pumpkin soup, and fried bananas. Fish is served almost every day and is topped with lots of fresh lime and hot pepper sauce. The people are mestizo, of "mixed blood," which means they are a mixture of Indian, African, and European ancestry.

6   ripe avocados, peeled, pitted, and cubed

1   14-ounce can heart of palm, drained and cubed

1   large red onion, thinly sliced into rings

4   sprigs fresh parsley, finely chopped

Lettuce leaves, for garnish

Tomato slices, for garnish

Lime wedges, for garnish

VINAIGRETTE:

¼   cup white wine vinegar

½   cup olive oil

¼   cup orange juice

1   sprig fresh basil, finely chopped

1   tablespoon dried thyme

2   tablespoons chopped white onion

2   green onions, finely chopped

2   sprigs fresh parsley, finely chopped

2   cloves garlic, minced

1   teaspoon salt

1   teaspoon freshly ground black pepper

1. In a large bowl, combine the avocados, heart of palm, red onion, and parsley. Toss lightly, being careful not to mash the avocados. Cover and refrigerate until ready to serve.

2. In a separate mixing bowl, whisk together all the ingredients for the vinaigrette until the oil and vinegar are well blended.

3. When you are ready to serve, add the vinaigrette to the avocado and palm and lightly toss. Serve over a bed of crisp lettuce and garnish with tomato slices and lime wedges. For more color, sprinkle the top of the salad with minced parsley or shredded carrots. This is great served with Coconut Shrimp (page 32).

Serves 6

HEART OF PALM FRITTERS

This dish incorporates a favorite island vegetable with a popular style of preparation. Fritters are, when prepared correctly, light and crispy. Dipped in a variety of hot sauces or chutneys, they make great appetizers and cocktail party treats.

1 cup flour

1 teaspoon baking powder

1 teaspoon salt

2 eggs, beaten

4 cloves garlic, minced

1 Scotch bonnet pepper, seeded and finely chopped

1 white onion, finely chopped

1 teaspoon freshly ground black pepper

2 sprigs fresh parsley, finely chopped

1 teaspoon dried thyme

1 14-ounce can heart of palm, drained and diced

¼ cup milk

Oil for deep frying

Lettuce leaves, for garnish

Lemon or lime wedges, for garnish

1. In a large mixing bowl, stir the flour and baking powder together. Add the salt, eggs, garlic, Scotch bonnet pepper, onion, black pepper, parsley, thyme, and heart of palm and fold together to form a stiff batter. Add the milk and stir well to form a dough. Cover and refrigerate for at least 1 hour. Properly covered and refrigerated, this dough will keep for 3 to 4 days.

2. Preheat a deep fryer to 400°F. Remove the dough and let it stand for 15 to 20 minutes. Drop by the tablespoonful into the hot oil and fry until golden brown. Be careful not to make the spoonfuls of batter too large or the dough may not cook in the center. Drain the fritters on paper towels and serve immediately on a platter covered with fresh lettuce. Garnish with lemon or lime wedges.

Serves 8 to 10

Appetizers & Salads

MARINATED CUCUMBER SALAD

This simple dish is found on just about every island and is very popular at Sugar Reef. We usually serve it with spicy dishes to refresh the palate. After a fiery mouthful, it's like a cool breeze on a hot day.

Martinique
Cruise ships are a popular sight off the shores of this lush tropical island. The scenery is diverse and includes volcanoes, waterfalls, tropical rainforests, and black beaches. A department of France, Martinique is very much French in character, with four-hour lunches, six-course meals, romance, and music. In fact, this island has its own special music called zouk, which is a unique blend of salsa and merengue or beguine. Like its sister island, Guadeloupe, Martinique is renowned for fine Creole and French cuisine. Many restaurants are converted private homes and present wonderful Caribbean ingredients cooked in the French style.

8   cucumbers, peeled and sliced (about 5 cups)
1   cup lime juice
1   cup white wine vinegar
1   red onion, thinly sliced
    Salt to taste
    Freshly ground black pepper to taste
2   tablespoons chopped fresh parsley
2   tablespoons chopped fresh coriander (optional)

In a large bowl, combine all the ingredients, cover, and refrigerate for at least 1 hour. The longer you marinate, the better.

Serves 10

CARIBBEAN FRUIT SALAD

The variety of fruits in the Caribbean is unmatched anywhere in the world. Unfortunately, not all of them are available in American markets, so we chose fruits for this recipe that should not be too hard to find.

1 medium pineapple, peeled, cored, and cubed

2 oranges, peeled and sectioned

1 grapefruit, peeled and sectioned

2 bananas, peeled and sliced ¼ inch thick

1 mango, peeled, pitted, and sliced into strips

1 papaya, peeled, seeded, and sliced into strips

Juice of 2 limes

2 tablespoons (1 ounce) white rum

½ cup shredded coconut

3 sprigs fresh mint, for garnish

In a large mixing bowl, combine all the fruits and lightly toss, being careful not to bruise or mash them. Add the lime juice and rum and mix in carefully. Cover and refrigerate until chilled. Just before serving, top the salad with the shredded coconut and garnish each serving with a mint leaf or two.

Serves 6

Appetizers & Salads

GREEN BANANAS VINAIGRETTE

The green banana is much like the ordinary potato when boiled. They are similar in texture and most definitely in flavor. In this recipe you boil the bananas until they are soft, then slice and top them with a tangy vinaigrette.

6 very green bananas

3 cloves garlic

1 red pepper, seeded and roughly chopped

1 green pepper, seeded and roughly chopped

1 teaspoon salt

1 teaspoon freshly ground black pepper

¼ cup white vinegar

Juice of 1 lime

¾ cup olive oil

1. In a large saucepan, bring 1 quart salted water to a brisk boil. Snip the ends off the bananas and add them to the boiling water. Let them boil, uncovered, for 45 minutes to 1 hour or until the skins begin to burst and the meat is tender. Drain and let cool at room temperature.

2. In a food processor, combine the garlic, red and green peppers, salt, pepper, vinegar, lime juice, and olive oil and puree until smooth.

3. Peel and slice the bananas and arrange on individual salad plates. Top each plate with the vinaigrette and serve immediately.

Serves 6

"Indians"

Columbus died a frustrated man. Throughout his life he was obsessed with finding a route to the Orient. He constantly misinterpreted the native people he found on the many islands of the Caribbean who tried to tell him, in a language he could not understand, that they were not the people he was looking for. In deference to his dream, Columbus called them Indians, which has survived to this day as our name for the native people of the Western Hemisphere.

CONGA PINEAPPLE AND CHICKEN SALAD

T his recipe gets its name from its snappy ingredients, which conjure up images of a conga line. Served in a pineapple bowl, it makes a very attractive luncheon meal.

1 large pineapple, halved lengthwise, including leaves

1 pound cooked chicken, cubed

3 cups cooked white rice

¼ cup golden raisins

¼ cup dark raisins

½ cup mango chutney, chopped

½ teaspoon ground nutmeg

½ teaspoon salt

½ teaspoon freshly ground black pepper

¾ cup mayonnaise

Chopped fresh parsley, for garnish

1. Carefully scoop out the meat from the pineapple halves, leaving a ½-inch-thick shell. Coarsely chop the pineapple meat.

2. In a large mixing bowl, combine the pineapple, chicken, rice, raisins, chutney, nutmeg, salt, pepper, and mayonnaise. Lightly toss until all the ingredients are mixed and coated with mayonnaise.

3. Fill each pineapple half with the salad and cover. Refrigerate for at least 30 minutes or until chilled. Garnish with parsley before serving.

Serves 6

Appetizers & Salads

CURRIED CHICKEN AND MANGO SALAD

Curry is widely used on all the islands. So is mango. Put the two together and you get a fantastic combination. This is an easy recipe: Make the sauce, add it to chicken and mango, and place on a bed of lettuce.

If you can't find the Matouk and Windmill hot sauces in your food market, we suggest you try our sauce recipes as substitutes.

2   6-ounce boneless chicken breasts, skin removed

1   cup mayonnaise

1½ teaspoons Matouk hot sauce or Sauce Ti-Malice (page 186)

1½ teaspoons Windmill hot sauce or Jackie's Hot Sauce (page 187)

1   chicken bouillon cube

3   tablespoons curry powder

2   cloves garlic, chopped

3   green onions, including green, chopped

2   sprigs fresh parsley, chopped

¼   cup canned mango nectar

1   teaspoon salt

1   teaspoon freshly ground black pepper

2   ripe mangoes, peeled, pitted, and sliced

Lettuce leaves, for garnish

Chopped fresh parsley, for garnish

1. Grill or pan-fry the chicken breasts until fully cooked. Cut into ½-inch cubes and set aside.

2. In a food processor or blender, combine the mayonnaise, hot sauces, bouillon cube, curry powder, garlic, green onions, parsley, mango nectar, salt, and pepper. Puree until the mixture is smooth and creamy.

3. In a large bowl, combine the chicken and the mango slices. Pour the curry sauce on top and lightly toss. Arrange lettuce leaves on individual salad plates, top with the chicken and mango, and garnish with parsley. Chill or serve immediately.

Serves 4

"JERK" CHICKEN SALAD

T he "Jerk" Chicken Sugar Reef Style (page 98) was so popular as a main course that we decided to lighten it up for a lunch salad. The delicate flavors of the vegetables are offset by the punch of the jerk spice for a contrast of flavors.

Appetizers & Salads

1 tablespoon ground allspice

1 tablespoon dried thyme

1½ teaspoons cayenne pepper

1½ teaspoons freshly ground black pepper

1 teaspoon ground nutmeg

1 teaspoon ground cinnamon

2 tablespoons salt

2 tablespoons garlic powder

1 tablespoon sugar

1 cup olive oil

½ cup white vinegar

½ cup orange juice

¼ cup soy sauce

Juice of 1 lime

1 Scotch bonnet pepper, seeded and finely chopped

1 cup chopped white onion

3 green onions, chopped

4 6-ounce boneless breasts of chicken

Lettuce leaves

3 carrots, sliced

1 small red onion, sliced

Tomato wedges, for garnish

Dill pickle slices, for garnish

Lime slices, for garnish

1. In a large mixing bowl, combine the allspice, thyme, cayenne pepper, black pepper, nutmeg, cinnamon, salt, garlic powder, and sugar. Mix together well and add the olive oil slowly, stirring with a wire whisk, then add the vinegar, orange juice, soy sauce, lime juice, Scotch bonnet pepper, white onion, and green onions. Place the chicken breasts in the marinade, cover, and refrigerate for at least 1 hour.

2. Preheat an outdoor grill until the coals are hot. Remove the chicken from the marinade and grill for 4 to 5 minutes per side or until fully cooked. While grilling, baste with the marinade, but be careful—the high oil content of the sauce will cause the coals to flame up. This makes the meat taste wonderful, as it sears in the flavors of the marinade, but do not overblacken. (This step can be done in an iron skillet over high heat.)

3. Prepare individual salad plates with lettuce, carrot slices, and red onion slices. Cut each breast into 3 or 4 pieces and arrange on the lettuce. Heat the marinade until bubbly and top each serving with 3 tablespoons. Garnish with tomato wedges, dill pickle slices, and a slice of lime.

Serves 4 to 6

COLD SEAFOOD SALAD

This main course salad successfully blends the fruits of the sea with the fruits of the land. Not only is it easy to prepare in advance, but it is beautiful to look at, making all the table decoration you need.

The Mango

There are many ways to eat a mango, but we suggest a technique known as "sucking mango" on several of the islands. First you massage the fruit until it is very soft. Then cut off the tip, place your mouth over the incision, and suck out the juices and pulp.

If you wish to halve a mango, it is no small challenge! Its pit is a furry seed in the shape of a flattened football (somewhat smaller, of course) and gives the fruit its oval form. Cut a generous lengthwise slice from one side, as close to the seed as possible. Turn the mango over, and cut a second large piece lengthwise. If you are lucky, you will have two servings of fruit, which can be eaten with a spoon.

½   **pound white lump crabmeat**

1   **pound medium shrimp, cooked and peeled**

1   **ripe mango, peeled, pitted, and sliced**

1   **orange, peeled and sectioned**

½   **green pepper, seeded and finely chopped**

1   **7-ounce can artichoke hearts, drained and halved**

1   **ripe avocado, peeled, pitted, and cubed**

4   **green onions, finely chopped**

1   **Scotch bonnet pepper, seeded and finely chopped**

½   **cup unsalted roasted cashews**

2   **teaspoons salt**

1   **teaspoon freshly ground black pepper**

    Juice of 1 lime

    Lettuce leaves, for garnish

1   **cup Avocado Mayonnaise (page 195)**

    Lime wedges, for garnish

1. Pick over the crabmeat to remove any bits of cartilage. In a large bowl, combine the shrimp, crabmeat, mango, orange, green pepper, artichoke hearts, avocado, green onions, Scotch bonnet pepper, cashews, salt, and black pepper. Lightly toss and sprinkle with freshly squeezed lime juice.

2. Arrange lettuce leaves on individual salad plates and spoon a portion of salad on top. Serve with Avocado Mayonnaise or any favorite salad dressing. Garnish with lime wedges.

Serves 6

CRABMEAT AVOCADO

This dish originated in the French West Indies. We have sampled several variations, but this one is by far the most delicious. It makes an impressive appetizer salad.

3   ripe avocados

1   pound white lump crabmeat

6   green onions, finely chopped

3   cloves garlic, minced

2   Scotch bonnet peppers, seeded and finely chopped

1   large white onion, finely chopped

4   sprigs fresh parsley, finely chopped

    Juice of 2 limes

2   tablespoons olive oil

1½   teaspoons salt

1½   teaspoons freshly ground black pepper

6   large lettuce leaves

1. Slice the avocados into halves and remove the pit. Scrape out most but not all of the avocado meat, creating a bowl, and set aside for later use.

2. Rinse the crabmeat well and shake off any excess water. Pick over to remove any cartilage.

3. In a large bowl, mash the avocado meat until smooth. Add the green onions, garlic, Scotch bonnet peppers, white onion, parsley, and lime juice and mix well. Add the crabmeat, olive oil, salt, and pepper and mix again until everything is well combined.

4. Place a lettuce leaf in each of the halved avocado shells. Fill the shells with the crabmeat mixture until all of it is used. Cover and refrigerate for at least 1 hour. Top each avocado with a light vinaigrette before serving.

Serves 6

Appetizers & Salads

CALYPSO SALAD

This specialty was created by our Caribbean chef to satisfy the lust New Yorkers have for great salads. Colorful and packed with flavor, it contains lots of fresh ingredients found on the islands of the Caribbean *and* Manhattan.

Coriander

In Spanish markets, this pungent herb is known as cilantro. It is used in spicy cuisine throughout the world and in fact is also called Chinese parsley both for its use in Chinese cooking and for its resemblance to flat-leafed Italian parsley. Usually sold with its roots intact, coriander can be stored in the refrigerator for up to a week. Just plunge the roots into a glass of water, cover with a plastic bag, and secure with a rubber band. Note that the flavor of fresh coriander in no way resembles that of coriander seed, so don't try it as a substitute.

AVOCADO DRESSING:

2   ripe avocados, peeled, pitted, and cubed

Juice of 2 limes

2   tablespoons orange juice

¼   cup olive oil

2   green onions, finely chopped

2   sprigs fresh coriander, chopped

1   teaspoon chopped Scotch bonnet pepper

1   teaspoon salt

1   teaspoon white pepper

1   pound large shrimp, cooked and peeled

1   14-ounce can heart of palm, rinsed, drained, and sliced

2   oranges, peeled and quartered

1   grapefruit, peeled and quartered

1   red onion, thinly sliced

2   green onions, finely chopped

Lettuce leaves

1. In a blender or food processor, puree all the ingredients for the avocado dressing until smooth and creamy. Transfer to a bowl, cover, and refrigerate until chilled.

2. In a large salad bowl, combine the shrimp, heart of palm, oranges, grapefruit, red onion, green onions, and lettuce leaves. Lightly toss and cover. Refrigerate until the salad has chilled. Serve on individual salad plates and top with the avocado dressing.

Serves 6

CONCH AND AVOCADO SALAD

Avocado is excellent in salads and is used a lot in the Caribbean. It works especially well with seafood and in this recipe is teamed with a marinated conch salad.

2 cups diced prepared conch meat (page 11)

1 white onion, finely chopped

1 green pepper, seeded and finely chopped

1 clove garlic, minced

1 teaspoon chopped fresh parsley

½ teaspoon dried oregano

½ cup olive oil

Juice of 3 limes

1 tablespoon white vinegar

1 teaspoon salt

½ teaspoon curry powder

½ teaspoon freshly ground black pepper

2 dashes hot red pepper sauce

2 ripe avocados

Lettuce leaves, for garnish

Lime slices, for garnish

1. In a large bowl, combine the conch, onion, green pepper, garlic, parsley, oregano, olive oil, lime juice, vinegar, salt, curry powder, black pepper, and hot sauce. Stir well, cover, and refrigerate overnight.

2. Just before serving, cut the avocados in half and remove the pits. Line 4 salad plates with lettuce leaves, place an avocado half on each, and stuff with a large scoop of the marinated conch. Garnish with lime slices and serve.

Serves 4

Appetizers & Salads

SCORCHED CONCH SALAD *(Bahamas)*

The Bahamas are known for many things, but especially for wonderful conch dishes. The many islands and cays are perfect hiding spots for this meaty delicacy. This dish is scorched with pepper rather than heat and eaten raw, seviche-style.

The Bahamas

Columbus discovered the Bahamas, which comprises 700 islands and 2,000 cays. Only 30 of these islands are inhabited; their history is colorful. Most of the inhabitants are descendants of loyalists and slaves who left America after the Revolution. Some were shipwrecked here. In the old days, rum running was commonplace, and the islands were a refuge for pirates, Spanish explorers, and Indians, who were lured by the turquoise waters and the exotic terrain. Locals enjoy a bounty of fresh conch, which is a delicacy here.

1 **pound prepared conch meat (page 11), diced**

1 **small tomato, diced**

1 **cucumber, peeled and diced**

1 **small red onion, finely chopped**

¼ **cup fresh lime juice (about 2 limes)**

6 **tablespoons orange juice**

1 **teaspoon freshly ground black pepper**

1 **teaspoon salt**

1 **Scotch bonnet pepper, seeded and finely chopped**

In a large mixing bowl, combine all the ingredients, stir well, and cover. Refrigerate at least 2 hours to marinate the ingredients. Serve cold as a side dish or appetizer.

Serves 4 to 5

COCONUT SHRIMP

Crispy shrimp, coconut, and eight different spices create a great taste sensation in this unusual starter. Or serve the shrimp as an entree with saffron rice.

1½ teaspoons sweet paprika

1½ teaspoons freshly ground black pepper

2 teaspoons salt

1 teaspoon garlic powder

1¾ teaspoons onion powder

1¾ teaspoons dried oregano, crumbled

1¾ teaspoons dried thyme, crumbled

1 tablespoon cayenne pepper

1 12-ounce bottle beer

1¾ cups flour

1 tablespoon baking soda

50 medium-size shrimp (about 2 pounds), peeled and deveined (leave on tails)

3 cups shredded unsweetened coconut (about 6 ounces)

Oil for deep frying

Lettuce leaves, for garnish

Hot red pepper sauce, for garnish

1. Thoroughly combine the paprika, black pepper, salt, garlic powder, onion powder, oregano, thyme, and cayenne pepper in a small bowl.

2. In a large bowl, combine the beer, flour, and baking soda and mix well with a wire whisk. (The batter should have the consistency of pancake batter.) Stir in the spice mixture, using a wire whisk.

3. Spread the coconut out on a plate. Dip each shrimp into the batter, shake off any excess, then roll in the coconut to cover. Press the shrimp in the palm of your hand to make the coconut flakes stick.

4. In a deep fryer or large saucepan, heat the oil to 350°F. Drop the shrimp, 6 at a time, into the hot oil and fry until golden brown, about 1 minute. Drain on paper towels and serve on a bed of fresh lettuce. Top with hot red pepper sauce if you like.

Serves 10 as an appetizer
Serves 5 as an entree

Appetizers & Salads

SHRIMP FRITTERS

Just about any seafood makes a great fritter, and shrimp is no exception. We serve the fritters with hot pepper sauce as well as fresh Mango Chutney Glaze. Be sure to slice up plenty of lemons and limes.

Fish Fritters

Accras, or fish fritters, are found on just about every island in the Caribbean in one form or another. On Dominica, a small indigenous fish called the ti ti-oui is used in fritters. Because it is tiny, the fish is used whole. On the Spanish-speaking islands the fritters are called bacalaitos and made with codfish. The traditional Jamaican akkra is made from ground black-eyed peas or soybeans and called stamp-and-go. On the Dutch islands the fritters are called cala and have a heavier batter, and on the French-speaking islands they are referred to as Acrat de morue. Any way you slice, dice, or fry, they are an extraordinary treat.

1 cup flour
1 teaspoon baking powder
1 teaspoon salt
2 eggs, beaten
4 cloves garlic, minced
1 Scotch bonnet pepper, seeded and finely chopped
1 medium white onion, finely chopped
1 teaspoon freshly ground black pepper
2 sprigs fresh parsley, finely chopped
1 teaspoon dried thyme
1 pound medium shrimp, peeled, deveined, and chopped
¼ cup beer
  Oil for deep frying
  Lettuce leaves, for garnish
  Lemon and lime wedges, for garnish

1. In a large bowl, sift together the flour, baking powder, and salt. Stir in the eggs, garlic, Scotch bonnet pepper, onion, black pepper, parsley, thyme, and shrimp. Fold these ingredients together to form a stiff batter. Add the beer and stir well. Cover and refrigerate for at least 1 hour (or up to 2 days).

2. In a deep fryer, heat the oil to 400°F. When hot, drop the batter by the tablespoonful and fry until the fritters are golden brown, about 5 minutes. Be careful not to make the fritters larger than a tablespoon or the batter will not cook in the center before browning. Drain on paper towels and arrange on large platters with lettuce leaves and wedges of lime and lemon. The fritters are terrific served with chilled Mango Chutney Glaze (page 191).

Serves 10 to 12

CONCH FRITTERS *(Bahamas)*

Tender, fresh, and fried to perfection—this is another good example of how well conch is prepared in the Bahamas, where it is a favorite delicacy.

1   **pound prepared conch meat (page 11), chopped**

2   **eggs, beaten**

4   **cloves garlic**

1   **green pepper, seeded**

1   **white onion**

2   **sprigs fresh parsley**

1   **cup flour**

1   **teaspoon baking powder**

1   **teaspoon salt**

1   **teaspoon freshly ground black pepper**

1   **teaspoon dried thyme**

¼   **cup milk**

    Oil for deep frying

    Lemon or lime wedges, for garnish

1. Put the conch in batches through a food processor until it is finely chopped. Transfer to a large bowl and stir in the eggs.

2. Place the garlic, green pepper, onion, and parsley through the food processor until finely chopped. Drain the vegetables in a sieve lined with cheesecloth, then add to the conch in the mixing bowl. Stir to combine the ingredients.

3. Stir the flour and baking powder together, then mix in with the other ingredients. Add the salt, pepper, thyme, and milk. Fold everything together to form a thick dough. Cover and refrigerate for at least 1 hour.

4. Preheat a deep fryer to 400°F. Remove the dough and let it stand for 15 to 20 minutes. Drop by the tablespoonful into the hot oil and fry until golden brown. Be careful not to make the spoonfuls of batter too large or the dough may not cook in the center. Drain the fritters on paper towels and serve immediately. Garnish with fresh lemon or lime wedges and serve with any of the Caribbean hot sauces on pages 186–189.

Serves 8

Appetizers & Salads

COD FRITTERS *(Dominican Republic)*

Almost every island we have visited or researched calls this dish its own, although by a variety of names. This particular rendition, from the Dominican Republic, is seasoned with fresh coriander and sweet green peppers.

1   cup flour

1   teaspoon baking powder

2   eggs, beaten

3   green onions, finely chopped

3   sprigs fresh coriander, finely chopped

2   sprigs fresh parsley, finely chopped

1   green pepper, seeded and finely chopped

1   red onion, finely chopped

1   white onion, finely chopped

4   cloves garlic, minced

1   tablespoon freshly ground black pepper

1   tablespoon dried oregano

2   tablespoons sweet paprika

2   tablespoons ground coriander

2   cups dried salt cod, prepared (page 11)

¼   cup milk (optional)

    Oil for deep frying

    Lemon or lime wedges, for garnish

1. In a large mixing bowl, stir the flour and baking powder together. Add the eggs, green onions, fresh coriander, parsley, green pepper, red and white onions, garlic, black pepper, oregano, paprika, ground coriander, and codfish. Mix the ingredients well to form a dough. Add the milk only if the batter is dry and not sticking together. Cover the bowl and refrigerate for at least 1 hour.

2. Preheat a deep fryer to 400°F. Remove the dough and let it stand for 15 to 20 minutes. Drop by the tablespoonful into the hot oil and fry until golden brown. Be careful not to make the spoonfuls of batter too large or the dough may not cook in the center. Drain the fritters on paper towels and serve immediately. Garnish with fresh lemon or lime wedges and serve with any of the Caribbean hot sauces on pages 186–189.

Serves 8 to 10

SALT COD WITH AVOCADO

The French name for this dish, *Feroce de Morue* (Fierce Salt Fish), describes it perfectly. The Scotch bonnet pepper and dominant flavor of the seared salt cod make for a fierce dish. It is most often served with calalou but is also excellent as an appetizer or salad.

½ pound dried salt cod, soaked in water to cover overnight

1 Scotch bonnet pepper, seeded and finely chopped

¼ cup olive oil

Juice of 1 lime

1 small white onion, thinly sliced

1 teaspoon freshly ground black pepper

2 ripe avocados, peeled, pitted, and sliced

Lime slices, for garnish

Scotch bonnet pepper slices, for garnish

1. Drain the salt cod and pat dry with paper towels. Place the fish in cheese-cloth and press out any remaining water. It must be thoroughly dry.

2. Heat a heavy iron skillet or an outdoor grill until very hot. Add the fish and grill until it is almost black and burned on both sides. Remove from the grill and pull off any skin and bones and discard. Break the fish into chunks or flakes.

3. In a large bowl, combine the salt cod with the Scotch bonnet pepper, olive oil, lime juice, onion, and black pepper. Toss the ingredients well and cover. Marinate for at least 1 hour, refrigerated.

4. Arrange the avocado slices on individual serving plates. Top with the cod and garnish with fresh lime and Scotch bonnet pepper slices.

Serves 4

Appetizers & Salads

LOBSTER GRATINÉE *(Haiti)*

The lobster in Haiti is as good as you will find anywhere in the Caribbean. This dish is a departure from the usual steamed or boiled version. The lobster is baked and topped with a light cream sauce and Gruyère cheese. It makes a great appetizer or light lunch with salad.

Juice of 1 lime
1 cup light cream
1 teaspoon salt
1 teaspoon freshly ground black pepper
2 pounds fresh lobster meat, cubed
½ cup grated Gruyère cheese
2 tablespoons bread crumbs
Lime slices, for garnish

1. Preheat the oven to 350°F. In a medium saucepan, combine the lime juice, cream, salt, and pepper. Heat until the sauce almost reaches the boiling point (do not let it come to a complete boil), stirring constantly with a wooden spoon.

2. Arrange the lobster meat in individual baking dishes and top with the sauce. Bake for 30 minutes or until the sauce is bubbly, then remove the dishes from the oven.

3. Increase the oven heat to broil. Sprinkle the cheese evenly over the lobster and top with the bread crumbs. Brown the topping under the broiler for 2 to 3 minutes and garnish each dish with a slice of fresh lime before serving.

Serves 6

Voodoo

Haiti is closely associated with voodoo, a religious cult that exists side by side with Catholicism and is the most vivid heritage that the slaves brought with them from Africa. It helped to ensure the continued existence of the African culture in the New World. The religion involves the worship of many gods and touches every part of Haitian life—music, art, and food.

Soups

LATIN CARROT SOUP *(Dominican Republic)*

Our chef brought us this wonderful soup from his homeland, the Dominican Republic. Don't let lack of access to annatto oil stop you from enjoying such a delicious combination of vegetables and herbs. You can substitute any vegetable oil.

¼ cup annatto oil or vegetable oil

1 white onion, chopped

3 cloves garlic, chopped

3 stalks celery, chopped

1 bunch carrots, sliced (about 5 to 6)

1 cup potatoes, peeled and cubed

4 cups chicken stock

Bouquet garni (1 green onion, 1 sprig fresh parsley, 1 sprig fresh thyme)

1½ cups heavy cream

1 tablespoon salt

1 tablespoon freshly ground black pepper

2 tablespoons ground cumin

1½ teaspoons ground sage

1½ teaspoons dried oregano

Garlic croutons, for garnish

1. Heat the oil in a large Dutch oven and sauté the onion, garlic, and celery for about 5 minutes or until tender. Add the carrots and potatoes and continue to sauté for another 5 to 10 minutes.

2. Add the chicken stock and bouquet garni. Bring the soup to a brisk boil, stirring well. Lower the heat and simmer, covered, for 20 minutes or until the carrots and potatoes are tender.

3. Remove the soup from the stove and discard the bouquet garni. In a food processor or blender, puree the soup along with the cream, salt, pepper, cumin, sage, and oregano until it has a smooth consistency.

4. Pour the soup back into the Dutch oven and simmer for another 10 to 15 minutes. Serve garnished with garlic croutons.

Serves 6

CREAM OF CALABAZA SOUP *(Jamaica)*

In Jamaica it is said that pumpkin soup "lifts up a man's soul and makes him prophesy." The hearty soups on this island are thickened with vegetables instead of cream and make meals in themselves. This is such a soup, great as a main course or as an appetizer. The pumpkin should be firm, and its meat a rich yellow color.

8   cups water

4   cups chicken stock

1   calabaza pumpkin, peeled and chopped

2   carrots, roughly chopped

1   white onion, roughly chopped

2   stalks celery, roughly chopped

Bouquet garni (2 sprigs fresh thyme, 2 sprigs fresh parsley, 1 bay leaf)

1   teaspoon salt

1   teaspoon freshly ground black pepper

1   cup heavy cream

2   tablespoons (1 ounce) dry sherry

Chopped fresh parsley, for garnish

1. Place the water, chicken stock, pumpkin, carrots, onion, celery, bouquet garni, salt, and pepper in a large stockpot and bring to a boil over high heat. Boil rapidly, uncovered, for about 15 minutes, then lower the heat and cover. Let the soup simmer, stirring occasionally, for 1 hour or until the vegetables are tender.

2. Remove the soup from the stove and discard the bouquet garni. Scoop out the vegetables with a slotted spoon and puree them in a food processor or blender. Ladle in some of the soup liquid until the puree has a smooth consistency. Add the heavy cream and quickly blend for about 15 seconds.

3. Return the puree to the liquid in the stockpot and heat over moderate heat, stirring well. Add the sherry and simmer for another 10 minutes. Garnish with parsley and serve immediately.

Serves 4 to 6

That's a Might Pretty Motion
Afro-American song

That's a might pretty motion Dee-di-dee.
That's a might pretty motion Dee-di-dee.
Rise sugar rise.

EDDO SOUP *(Barbados)*

The eddo, sometimes referred to as coco, is a hairy root vegetable about the size of a potato. It tastes much like a potato too but is a bit more starchy. Soup is the most popular way to use eddoes in Barbados.

½ pound salt pork, cubed

2 white onions, finely chopped

1 pound eddoes or potatoes, peeled and cubed

1 teaspoon salt

1 teaspoon freshly ground black pepper

8 cups water

Bouquet garni (3 sprigs fresh thyme, 3 sprigs fresh parsley, 3 green onions)

2 tablespoons butter

3 sprigs fresh parsley, finely chopped

1. In a heavy Dutch oven, brown the salt pork, stirring well, then add the chopped onions. Let the onions sauté in the pork drippings until they become limp. Add the eddoes, salt, pepper, and water, stir well to mix, then add the bouquet garni. Let the soup come to a brisk boil, lower the heat, and simmer, covered, for 30 minutes or until the eddoes are tender.

2. Remove the soup from the stove and discard the bouquet garni. Puree the soup in a food processor until smooth and creamy. Return to the Dutch oven and heat thoroughly. Stir in the butter and chopped parsley before serving.

Serves 6 to 8

Soups

SPICED GROUNDNUT SOUP

 Groundnut is another name for the peanut, which originated in Africa. This recipe is also African in origin and was brought to the Caribbean by slaves. It is a mainstay in both places.

¼ cup vegetable oil

1 small white onion, finely chopped

1 16-ounce jar unsweetened peanut butter

1 6-ounce can evaporated milk

¾ cup whole milk

6 cups hot water

2 tablespoons white pepper

1 tablespoon cayenne pepper

¾ cup cooking sherry

1. In a heavy saucepan, heat the oil and sauté the onion until it is translucent. Stir in the peanut butter and stir constantly until it begins to melt and is completely combined with the onion, about 5 minutes.

2. Add the evaporated milk and whole milk and continue to stir. Just before the mixture begins to simmer, add the hot water and keep stirring. When the soup begins to simmer, add the white pepper, cayenne pepper, and sherry and stir well.

3. Lower the heat, cover, and simmer for 30 minutes, stirring occasionally. Serve immediately.

Serves 6 to 8

LENTIL SOUP *(Jamaica)*

I n the tropics, eating a big meal in the middle of the day can wipe you out, and a hearty soup that fills you up is a popular alternative. This is also the perfect soup for a cold winter day.

½ pound smoked sausage, finely chopped

3 stalks celery, finely chopped

2 green onions, finely chopped

1 yellow onion, finely chopped

1 red onion, finely chopped

3 sprigs fresh parsley, finely chopped

1 pound dried lentils, soaked overnight and drained

2 carrots, sliced

3½ cups chicken stock

2 cups water

½ cup dry white wine

2 sprigs fresh thyme

1 tablespoon dried oregano

4 teaspoons salt

4 teaspoons freshly ground black pepper

1. In a large Dutch oven, brown the sausage until it renders fat. Add the celery, green onions, yellow and red onions, and parsley and sauté until limp. Add the remaining ingredients and bring the soup to a boil over medium heat, stirring well. Lower the heat and simmer, covered, for 2 hours or until the lentils are tender.

2. Remove 1 cup of the cooked lentils and mash until very soupy. Return to the pot and simmer the soup another 5 to 10 minutes, stirring constantly. Serve immediately or reheat for later use.

Serves 4 to 6

Soups

BLACK BEAN SOUP *(Cuba)*

The Cubans are masters with black beans, and this rich soup is a prime example. It combines an array of spices and ingredients and makes a great meal in itself.

Pirates

The word buccaneer comes from an Arawak Indian word, buocan. (A boucan is a wooden grilling platform on which meats are cooked.) Pirates were men of all nationalities and backgrounds and were united by the fact that they were fugitives. Most preyed upon merchant ships carrying goods between the islands and Europe. The most heavily attacked were the Spanish, whose boats were often laden with gold, precious stones, and spices. In fact, piracy greatly contributed to the demise of the Spanish in the New World by depriving the king of the wealth needed for power. Often pirates would flee to unknown islands for safety and bury their stolen goods until search parties gave up looking for them.

1½ pounds dried black beans, soaked overnight and drained

4 cups chicken stock

4 cups water

4 sprigs fresh coriander, finely chopped

2 cloves garlic, minced

1 red onion, finely chopped

1 green pepper, seeded and finely chopped

2 tablespoons salt

2 tablespoons freshly ground black pepper

2 tablespoons ground cumin

2 tablespoons dried oregano

1 Scotch bonnet pepper, seeded and finely chopped

1 whole orange

10 whole cloves

1 hard-cooked egg, peeled and mashed, for garnish

1. Place the beans in a heavy stockpot or Dutch oven and cover with the stock and water. Bring to a boil over moderate heat, then lower the heat to simmer and stir. Cover and cook the beans for about 1 hour or until they soften.

2. Remove 1 cup of the cooked beans and mash until very soupy. Return to the pot along with the coriander, garlic, onion, green pepper, salt, black pepper, cumin, oregano, and Scotch bonnet pepper. Stick the orange with the cloves and add to the beans. Stir all the ingredients together well.

3. Bring the beans back to a boil over moderate heat and stir well. Lower the heat, cover, and simmer for approximately 30 minutes.

4. Remove the orange and serve. Garnish with a sprinkle of hard-cooked egg or chopped red onion.

Serves 8

PEPPER SOUP

Strong ties between the cuisine of Africa and the Caribbean remain today. The two places are far apart geographically, yet closely connected in cuisine and culture, despite the years that have gone by since the first Africans landed on Caribbean sands. This soup is an example of the similarities in cooking styles.

1 3-pound chicken, cut into serving pieces

6 cups chicken stock

1 white onion, finely chopped

2 carrots, finely chopped

2 cloves garlic, minced

2 stalks celery, finely chopped

1 bay leaf

1 sprig fresh parsley, finely chopped

2 teaspoons salt

10 peppercorns

½ fresh coconut, grated

1 cup cooked chickpeas (or 1 8-ounce can, drained)

¼ cup butter

6 tablespoons flour

3 tablespoons ground turmeric

1 teaspoon ground ginger

1 teaspoon ground coriander

1 teaspoon cayenne pepper

1 cup heavy cream

Lemon slices, for garnish

1. In a Dutch oven, combine the chicken, chicken stock, onion, carrots, garlic, celery, bay leaf, parsley, salt, and peppercorns. Bring the mixture to a brisk boil, stirring occasionally. Lower the heat and let the soup simmer for 45 minutes or until the chicken pieces are tender.

2. Remove the Dutch oven from the stove and strain the soup, reserving the stock in one bowl and the chicken in another. Discard the bay leaf and any bits of vegetables. Briefly set the chicken aside and try to keep it warm. Pour the stock into a blender or food processor and add the grated coconut. Process for 1 minute and strain back into the bowl. Discard any remaining bits of coconut. Pour the stock back into the blender or food processor and add the chickpeas. Process for another minute or until the peas are thoroughly pureed. Briefly set aside.

3. Place the Dutch oven back on the stove, add the butter, and melt over low heat. Slowly add the flour, turmeric, ginger, coriander, and cayenne pepper, stirring until the ingredients are thoroughly combined. Slowly pour in the soup stock in a steady stream and continue to stir. Add the cream and the chicken pieces and stir well. Simmer the soup until hot and serve in individual bowls with piping hot white rice. Garnish each bowl with a slice of lemon and serve immediately.

Serves 4 to 6

CALLALOO *(Trinidad)*

Callaloo, calaloo, callilu, calalou, callau—this popular leafy vegetable indigenous to the Caribbean is much like the more familiar kale or spinach. A soup bearing its name is a staple on most every island but varies in consistency and style.

Gumbo-Callaloo Connection

Stews were common in Africa, where they were used to stretch meats and feed a lot of people. Many greens were added to give the stews more substance and body and the dish came to be known as callaloo. *In Louisiana gumbo is a popular stew that combines seafood, sausage, herbs, and okra in a thick and hearty dish served in large bowls with rice. The French and Spanish who settled regions of the Caribbean also went to Louisiana and had Africans in their kitchens. These Africans brought with them their traditions and styles of cooking. Gombo is an African word for okra and is remarkably similar to the popular Caribbean dish* callaloo.

2 **pounds fresh kale or spinach, stems removed**

¼ **pound salt pork, cut into ¼-inch strips**

½ **pound boneless lean pork, cut into ½-inch cubes**

2 **white onions, cut in half and thinly sliced**

Freshly ground black pepper to taste

4 **teaspoons hot red pepper sauce or to taste**

1 **tablespoon dried thyme, crumbled**

6 **cups well-flavored chicken stock**

½ **pound fresh white crabmeat**

1. Rinse the kale thoroughly, pat dry with paper towels, and roughly chop; set aside.

2. Place the salt pork strips in a large Dutch oven and sauté over medium heat for 10 minutes or until they are brown and the fat has been rendered.

3. Drain off all but 2 tablespoons of the fat. Add the pork cubes and onions to the Dutch oven and sauté until the pork is brown and the onions are translucent, about 5 minutes.

4. Add half the chopped kale, several grinds of black pepper, the red pepper sauce, thyme, and chicken stock. When the first batch of kale has wilted considerably, about 5 minutes, add the remainder. Cover and simmer about 2½ hours.

5. Remove the salt pork strips. Add the crabmeat and stir to mix in. Cover and continue simmering another 5 minutes. May be served immediately but is better if made in advance and reheated before serving. Serve with white rice or boiled plantains.

Serves 6 to 8

CRAB BISQUE

T his rich soup, a Caribbean variation on the classic French recipe, combines fresh crabmeat with sweet peppers, carrots, mushrooms, and more. An excellent opener for any meal, it is, not surprisingly, especially popular on the French islands.

¼ cup olive oil

2 stalks celery, finely chopped

½ cup chopped green pepper

½ cup chopped red pepper

½ cup chopped white onion

2 green onions, finely chopped

1 cup chopped carrots

½ cup chopped mushrooms

½ teaspoon salt

½ teaspoon freshly ground black pepper

3 cups fish stock

Bouquet garni (2 sprigs fresh rosemary, 2 sprigs fresh mint, 2 sprigs fresh parsley, 1 bay leaf)

1 pound lump white crabmeat, rinsed and drained

1 cup heavy cream

½ cup bottled or fresh clam juice

¼ cup dry sherry

Chopped fresh parsley, for garnish

1. In a Dutch oven, heat the olive oil and sauté the celery, green and red peppers, white onion, and green onions until they are limp. Add the carrots, mushrooms, salt, black pepper, fish stock, bouquet garni, and bay leaf and bring to a brisk boil. Lower the heat, cover, and simmer the soup for 20 minutes or until the carrots are tender.

2. Remove the soup from the stove and discard the bouquet garni. Pour the soup through a strainer, reserving both the liquid and the vegetables. In a food processor, puree the vegetables along with ½ cup of the soup liquid. When smooth, add the crabmeat and puree until completely smooth.

3. Return the puree and soup liquid to the Dutch oven. Bring the soup to a simmer over low heat, stirring constantly. Add the heavy cream and stir well, then the clam juice. Let this simmer for about 20 minutes, covered, stirring occasionally.

4. Add the sherry and stir well. Leave the bisque on low heat, uncovered, for another 5 minutes. Garnish with parsley and serve.

Serves 4 to 6

CREAMED COCO CONCH CHOWDER

This recipe calls for coconut cream. It is available as a commercial product in specialty markets, but be sure to get the unsweetened kind. The hot pepper, although optional, is highly recommended, as it heightens the unusual combination of flavors in this typically Caribbean soup.

¼ cup coconut oil

1 pound prepared conch meat (page 11), diced

1 small white onion, chopped

1 stalk celery, chopped

2 cloves garlic, minced

½ green pepper, seeded and chopped

1 quart water

3 green plantains, peeled and sliced

2 tablespoons salt

1 8-ounce can evaporated milk

3 tablespoons coconut cream (page 10)

1 tablespoon ground allspice

½ tablespoon chopped Scotch bonnet pepper (optional)

1 tablespoon white pepper

1 tablespoon ground nutmeg

¼ cup grated unsweetened coconut

3 ounces dry sherry

⅓ cup flour (optional)

Chopped green onion, for garnish

1. In a Dutch oven, heat the coconut oil and sauté the conch, onion, celery, garlic, and green pepper until the vegetables are soft, about 10 minutes. Stir constantly to prevent sticking.

2. Add the water, plantains, and salt and stir well. Bring the water to a boil, lower the heat, and let the plantains simmer, covered, until they are tender, about 30 to 40 minutes.

3. Remove the Dutch oven from the stove and drain off and save the liquid for later use. Place the solids in a food processor with ¼ cup of the liquid and puree. When smooth, return to the Dutch oven along with the reserved liquid.

4. Bring the soup to a simmer over medium heat. Stirring slowly, add the evaporated milk, coco cream, allspice, Scotch bonnet pepper, white pepper, nutmeg, and coconut. Let the soup cook for 10 minutes, stirring occasionally, then add the sherry and heat for another 10 to 15 minutes. If a thicker soup is desired, you can blend the flour with a small amount of water and add to the soup. Garnish with chopped green onion and more grated coconut.

Serves 6

FISH SOUP

Soups tend to be heartier in the Caribbean than one might expect in a hot climate. The idea is to eat a filling meal without weighing oneself down with multiple courses. For this main course soup, the fresher the ingredients, the better. Clams may be substituted for the oysters.

½ cup olive oil

1 carrot, finely chopped

2 white onions, finely chopped

2 cloves garlic, minced

2 leeks, finely chopped

6 cups fish stock

2 tomatoes, peeled and chopped

1 bay leaf

½ pound kingfish fillets, cut into pieces

1 cup dry white wine

Juice of 1 lime

1 cup chopped raw shrimp

12 shucked oysters

½ cup chopped pimiento

1 teaspoon salt

Pinch cayenne pepper

1 teaspoon freshly ground black pepper

1 loaf fresh French or Cuban bread

Butter

Chopped parsley, for garnish

1. In a Dutch oven, heat the olive oil over moderate heat and sauté the carrot, onions, garlic, and leeks until they become golden brown. Add the fish stock, tomatoes, bay leaf, and fish, stirring well. Lower the heat and simmer for about 40 minutes, stirring occasionally.

2. Stir in the wine, lime juice, shrimp, oysters, pimiento, salt, cayenne pepper, and black pepper. Stir well and continue to simmer until the shrimp turn pink and the oysters are cooked, about 10 minutes.

3. Slice the bread into rounds and butter each slice. Toast under the broiler until crispy and brown. Before serving the soup, place a slice or two of the toast in the bottom of each soup bowl and pour the hot soup on top. Garnish with the chopped parsley and serve immediately.

Serves 6

Soups

CUCUMBER YOGURT SOUP *(Haiti)*

This cold soup reflects more of the African than French Creole influences on Haiti. The delicate blending of herbs gives it a light and fresh taste—perfect on a hot day.

Haiti

The Arawak name means "mountainous" and adequately describes the terrain of this island country, which occupies the western third of Hispaniola, next to the Dominican Republic. Although French is the official language, most native people speak a Creole dialect that is a combination of French, African, and Indian.

Due to current political and economic problems, tourism to Haiti is almost nonexistent. This is too bad because it has many beautiful attractions. The food of Haiti brilliantly combines French with Creole West Indian and African elements. The seafood is excellent, and Haitian specialties include grilled lobster with Creole sauce, fried pork, bananas flambé, and coconut pudding.

3 cups plain yogurt

2 cups milk

1 cup heavy cream

3 tablespoons olive oil

1 tablespoon white vinegar

2 cups grated peeled cucumber

2 tablespoons finely chopped leek

1 tablespoon chopped fresh thyme

1 tablespoon chopped fresh dill

1 tablespoon chopped fresh marjoram

1 tablespoon chopped fresh tarragon

1 tablespoon chopped fresh mint

1 tablespoon chopped fresh basil

1 tablespoon white pepper

1 teaspoon salt

In a large mixing bowl, whisk together the yogurt, milk, and heavy cream. Slowly whisk in the olive oil and vinegar until smooth and creamy, then add the cucumber and leek, stirring well to combine. Season the soup with the herbs, pepper, and salt and stir well. When all the ingredients are well combined, cover and refrigerate the soup until completely chilled, about 1 hour.

Serves 4 to 6

COLD CURRY SOUP

This recipe, by far one of the easiest in the cookbook, found its way to the Caribbean from Africa. Served chilled, it makes a refreshing starter after a hot day at the beach.

1 cup chicken stock
½ cup plain yogurt
1 10½-ounce can condensed cream of mushroom soup
2 tablespoons curry powder
2 tablespoons finely chopped fresh chives

In a food processor or blender, combine all the ingredients and blend for 1 minute. Place in a serving bowl, cover, and refrigerate until very cold.

Serves 4

Soups

COLD AVOCADO SOUP

The delicate flavor of the avocado is greatly enhanced in a puree or soup. This makes a light and refreshing opener to a luncheon or summer evening meal.

2 ripe avocados, peeled, pitted, and cubed
½ cup sour cream
½ cup heavy cream
3 green onions, finely chopped
   Juice of 3 limes
¾ cup chicken stock
1 teaspoon freshly ground black pepper
1 teaspoon salt
   Lime wedges, for garnish
   Chopped fresh parsley, for garnish

Puree all the ingredients in a food processor or blender until smooth and creamy. Pour the soup into a large serving bowl, cover, and refrigerate for at least 30 minutes. Garnish each serving with a lime wedge and chopped parsley.

Serves 4

Nevis

Europeans came to this island in the nineteenth century to experience the wonderful mineral waters on Cades Bay, which give it the reputation of Spa of the Islands. Columbus discovered the island in 1493 and named it Nieves, which means "snows" in Spanish, because of the numerous clouds surrounding its high mountain peaks. The island has endless stretches of sandy beaches and a lagoon that looks like it is right out of South Pacific. Nevis is quaint and old-fashioned and the people are quite friendly. It could easily become a big resort, but the people refuse to give in to developers and fight to maintain the rural charm and remoteness of their island.

FISH STOCK

T his basic stock is called for in many of the recipes. It can be made in advance and stored in the refrigerator or frozen until you need it.

6 cups water

2 pounds fish bones, including heads and tails

1 white onion, chopped

Bouquet garni (4 sprigs fresh parsley, 2 sprigs fresh thyme, 2 green onions, 1 bay leaf)

1 teaspoon salt

1 teaspoon freshly ground black pepper

1. In a Dutch oven, bring the water, fish bones, onion, bouquet garni, salt, and pepper to a boil. Reduce the heat, cover, and simmer, stirring occasionally, for 30 minutes.

2. Remove the stock from the stove and discard the bouquet garni, bones, and other solids. Strain the stock, place in storage containers, and refrigerate or freeze until ready to use.

Yield: 5½ cups

Soups

CHICKEN STOCK

Good stock is essential to many a dish—soups, stews, sauces, and more. This one is good as a vegetable soup if not strained. Make it in advance and store in the refrigerator or freezer until you are ready to use.

6   quarts water

1   chicken carcass

3   carrots, roughly chopped

3   stalks celery, roughly chopped

1   large white onion, quartered

3   allspice berries

2   bay leaves

1   Scotch bonnet pepper, whole

1   teaspoon salt

1   teaspoon freshly ground black pepper

3   sprigs fresh thyme

3   sprigs fresh parsley

1. Bring the water to a boil in a large stockpot and add all the remaining ingredients. Let the soup boil rapidly for 10 to 15 minutes, stirring occasionally, then lower the heat and cover. Simmer for 2 to 3 hours, stirring occasionally.

2. Remove the stock from the stove and discard the vegetables and bones. Strain if you want a clear broth. It can be stored in the refrigerator for 3 to 4 days.

Yield: 12 cups

Seafood

BAKED RED SNAPPER

Visually, this is one of the prettiest dishes we have prepared. It is also one of the best tasting. Banana leaves add to both the appearance and the flavor but can be difficult to find. Try the frozen foods section of specialty markets, where we have found them on occasion. If you have no luck, foil is an acceptable alternative.

1 4- to 5-pound red snapper, with head and tail, cleaned and scaled

Juice of 1 lime

5 tablespoons butter

2 strips bacon, chopped

4 cloves garlic, minced

1 white onion, finely chopped

4 green onions, finely chopped

2 sprigs fresh parsley, finely chopped

1 green pepper, seeded and finely chopped

1 Scotch bonnet pepper, seeded and finely chopped (optional)

1 tomato, cubed

½ teaspoon dried thyme

½ teaspoon dried marjoram

1 teaspoon salt

1 teaspoon freshly ground black pepper

2 tablespoons red wine

½ cup bread crumbs

¼ cup dark rum

1 large banana leaf or aluminum foil

Sprigs of parsley, for garnish

Tomato slices, for garnish

Orange slices, for garnish

1. Rinse the fish and pat it dry inside and out. Squeeze lime juice all over it and cover. Refrigerate until ready for use.

2. In a heavy iron skillet, melt ¼ cup of the butter. Add the bacon and fry over moderate heat for about 4 minutes. Add the garlic, white onion, green onions, parsley, green pepper, and Scotch bonnet pepper. Let this sauté until the vegetables are tender, stirring occasionally. Add the tomato, thyme, marjoram, salt, black pepper, wine, and bread crumbs and stir to combine the ingredients thoroughly. Let this simmer, stirring constantly, for about 1 minute. Add the rum, stir, and simmer another few minutes. Remove the stuffing from the stove and let it cool. Preheat the oven to 375°F.

3. Place the fish on top of the banana leaf or foil. Stuff with the filling and dot the top with the remaining tablespoon of butter. Fold over the leaf or foil to seal the fish and bake for 1 hour. Transfer the fish to a serving platter, along with the banana leaf (discard foil if used). Garnish the platter with whole sprigs of parsley surrounding the fish. Top the fish with slices of tomato and orange.

Serves 4

POISSON ROUGE AVEC SAUCE LANGOUSTE *(Guadeloupe)*

Chefs in the French West Indies are masters of sauces. This one, an uncomplicated vinaigrette packed with flavor, gets its name from its color, not because it is prepared with lobster. Redfish or grouper can be used in place of the red snapper.

Guadeloupe

In Guadeloupe, eating out is the national pastime, and more than 100 restaurants cater not only to tourists but to locals as well. Every year in mid-August the Festival of Cooks highlights the mastery of the Societé des Cuisinieres, which comprises the island's elite women chefs. Each chef (there are about 200) prepares her best dish and dresses in a native costume of madras, complete with headdress and lots of gold jewelry. They carry elaborately decorated baskets filled with the island's specialties and trimmed with cooking utensils, which are blessed in a high mass. Afterward, they parade through the streets to a special hall where they celebrate all day.

4   6- to 8-ounce red snapper fillets

1¼ cups lime juice

½   cup white vinegar

½   cup finely chopped fresh parsley

1   cup finely chopped green onion

¼   cup chopped white onion

½   cup minced garlic

1¼ cups vegetable oil

    Salt to taste

    Freshly ground black pepper to taste

2   tablespoons finely chopped Scotch bonnet pepper

1   6-ounce can tomato paste

    Flour for coating fish

    Lime slices, for garnish

    Tomato slices, for garnish

1. Marinate the red snapper fillets in the lime juice for at least 1 hour at room temperature.

2. In a large bowl, combine the vinegar, parsley, green onions, white onion, and garlic. Slowly whisk in 1 cup of the oil, then add the salt, black pepper, Scotch bonnet pepper, and tomato paste. Whisk the ingredients until the oil and vinegar are thoroughly combined. Taste the sauce. If it is too hot, add another ¼ cup lime juice to cut the bite of the peppers. Set aside.

3. Remove the fish from the marinade and lightly coat each fillet with flour. In a large heavy skillet, heat the remaining oil over moderately high heat. Add the fish, 2 fillets at a time, and sauté for 4 minutes on each side or until golden brown.

4. Pat any excess oil from the fish with paper towels and arrange on warm serving plates. Spoon a generous amount of the sauce over the fish and garnish each plate with a slice of lime and a slice of tomato. Serve with Island Yams (page 150) and green beans.

Serves 4

BLAFF DU POISSON

T he name of this recipe supposedly mimics the sound the fish makes when it hits the boiling water. The fish is poached in a delicately seasoned broth that enhances the flavor without overpowering it. The traditional side dish is boiled green plantains or potatoes.

MARINADE:

- 2 cloves garlic, minced
- 1 tablespoon dried thyme
- 1 teaspoon salt
- 1 teaspoon freshly ground black pepper

  Juice of 4 limes

- 2 3-pound fish (red snapper, trout, grouper, or red perch), with head and tail, cleaned and scaled
- ¾ cup water
- ¼ cup white wine

  Bouquet garni (3 green onions, 3 sprigs fresh parsley, 2 sprigs fresh thyme, 1 bay leaf)

- 2 allspice berries
- 1 tablespoon freshly ground black pepper
- 1 whole Scotch bonnet pepper (optional)
- 1 small white onion, finely chopped

1. In a large bowl, combine the marinade ingredients and stir well to blend. Place the fish in the marinade and turn to coat them completely. Cover and refrigerate for at least 1 hour.

2. In a large saucepan or skillet, heat the water and wine until it comes to a brisk boil. Lower the heat and add the bouquet garni, allspice, black pepper, Scotch bonnet pepper, and onion. Let this simmer for about 15 minutes, stirring occasionally.

3. Add the fish and poach until they are tender and flake easily with a fork, about 10 minutes. Discard the bouquet garni and allspice and serve in individual soup bowls with the broth.

Serves 2

Seafood

BAJAN KINGFISH *(Barbados)*

T he recipe for this unusual dish, credited to Barbados alone, comes from our busboy Bismark Stanton's mother. When we introduced Bajan Kingfish, it was such a hit that it quickly became a permanent addition to the menu. The steaks are stuffed on each side with a delectable assortment of spices and vegetables, then lightly floured and deep-fried.

Bread In The Oven Baking
Jamaican children's song

Bread in the oven baking, baking, baking.
Bread in the oven baking, baking 'til the morning.
Then while ole massa sleeping, sleeping, sleeping.
While ole massa sleeping, sleeping 'til the morning.
See my little sister call her.
See my little sister fan her.
See my little sister turn her.
See my little sister wheel her.

5   green onions, finely chopped

2   white onions, chopped

1   green pepper, seeded and chopped

3   cloves garlic, minced

1½   teaspoons finely chopped Scotch bonnet pepper

1   tablespoon crushed fresh thyme

¼   cup lime juice

½   teaspoon salt

    Freshly ground black pepper to taste

4   6- to 8-ounce kingfish steaks, about 1 inch thick

    Flour for coating fish

    Oil for deep frying

1. In a bowl, combine the green onions, white onions, green pepper, garlic, Scotch bonnet pepper, thyme, lime juice, salt, and pepper.

2. Lay each kingfish steak flat and, with a sharp knife, make a horizontal incision on both sides, forming 2 pockets. Stuff the pockets with as much onion and pepper mixture as possible and lightly coat each steak with flour.

3. In a deep fryer or large saucepan, heat the oil to 350°F and fry each steak for 5 to 7 minutes or until golden. Handle carefully to prevent the stuffing from falling out of the fish. Drain. Serve with Calabaza Pumpkin Rice (page 152), Smothered Cabbage (page 139), and fresh cucumber salad.

Serves 4

PAN-FRIED GROUPER WITH CREOLE SAUCE

This recipe combines two popular foods in the Caribbean. Grouper is a fish common to most shores, and Creole sauces are served over just about everything. We have united the two with great results.

4   6- to 8-ounce grouper fillets

1¼   cups lime juice

    Flour for coating fish

    Oil for frying

    Lime slices, for garnish

CREOLE SAUCE:

¼   cup olive oil

2   green peppers, seeded and finely chopped

1   white onion, finely chopped

1   8-ounce can tomato sauce

½   cup white wine

1   teaspoon freshly ground black pepper

½   teaspoon salt

1   teaspoon dried thyme

1   teaspoon dried basil

1   teaspoon finely chopped Scotch bonnet pepper (optional)

1. Place the fish fillets in the lime juice, cover, and refrigerate for at least 1 hour.

2. In a heavy saucepan, make the Creole sauce. Heat the olive oil and sauté the green peppers and onion until they become limp. Add the tomato sauce, white wine, black pepper, salt, thyme, basil, and Scotch bonnet pepper and stir well. Let the sauce come to a boil, lower the heat, and simmer for 15 to 20 minutes, stirring occasionally.

3. Remove the fillets from the marinade and lightly coat with flour. Heat ½ inch of oil in a heavy skillet and fry the fish for about 6 minutes on each side; drain on paper towels. Place the fillets on individual serving plates and top with the Creole sauce. Garnish with slices of lime and serve immediately.

Serves 4

BAXTER ROAD FRIED FISH *(Barbados)*

Some of the finest fried fish anywhere is found on Baxter Road in Barbados. At about midnight on a Friday or Saturday this bustling street is transformed into an open-air marketplace where street vendors prepare fried fish in heavy iron skillets over large wood fires. People line up for the fish, served hot right out of the pan and wrapped in brown paper. What makes it so extraordinary are the hidden pockets of spice that burst open with every bite.

1   **bunch green onions**

1   **green pepper, seeded and roughly chopped**

1   **large white onion, roughly chopped**

4   **cloves garlic**

6   **sprigs fresh parsley or coriander**

¼   **cup dried marjoram**

2   **tablespoons dried thyme**

   Juice of 2 limes

1   **teaspoon salt**

1   **teaspoon freshly ground black pepper**

6   **6- to 8-ounce kingfish, flying fish, swordfish, or halibut fillets**

   Oil for frying

1   **egg, beaten**

   Bread crumbs for coating fish

   Lime wedges, for garnish

1. Place the green onions, green pepper, white onion, garlic, parsley, marjoram, thyme, and lime juice in a food processor and process to make a paste. Sprinkle the salt and pepper over the fish fillets, then rub liberally with the paste. If the fillets are thick enough, cut little pockets and stuff with the paste.

2. Heat ½ inch of oil in a heavy iron skillet. Dip each fillet into the beaten egg and coat with bread crumbs. Fry the fish until golden brown, about 4 minutes on each side. Drain on paper towels and serve immediately, garnished with fresh lime wedges.

Serves 6

TRENDY WRAPPED FISH

In New York there are many trends in style, particularly in fashion. Our chef has dressed this fish in the latest in fish wear—banana leaves. First the fish is lightly marinated, then delicately wrapped and baked or grilled. What makes this dish so special is the wonderful flavor the banana leaves impart to the fish without overpowering it. You can use foil if you are unable to find banana leaves.

MARINADE:

½ cup chicken stock

½ cup white vinegar

Juice of 1 lime

1 small white onion, finely chopped

½ green pepper, seeded and chopped

1 Scotch bonnet pepper, seeded and chopped

2 cloves garlic, minced

1 teaspoon salt

1 teaspoon freshly ground black pepper

1 teaspoon sweet paprika

1 teaspoon ground coriander

4 6-ounce fish fillets (red perch, sea trout, or grouper)

4 teaspoons butter

4 banana leaves (or 6 × 8-inch sheets of foil)

1. In a large bowl, combine all the ingredients for the marinade and mix well. Add the fish fillets, cover, and marinate in the refrigerator for at least 1 hour.

2. Preheat the oven to 350°F and remove the fish from the marinade. Spread a teaspoon of butter on each banana leaf or foil section. Lay a fillet on each leaf and top with about ¼ cup of the marinade. Wrap the fillets, using string to tie the banana leaves, and bake for 30 minutes or until the fish is fully cooked.

Serves 4

Seafood

GRILLED BANANA FLOUNDER *(Antigua)* ✓

This dish successfully blends the sweet flavor of ripe banana with the smoky flavor of fresh bacon. Add flounder and it's a winning combination. The fish can be grilled outdoors or baked in the oven.

Antigua

This island's claim to fame is its 365 beaches, one for every day of the year! It is an island carved out of limestone and volcanic rock and was named by Christopher Columbus after the Santa Maria la Antigua of Seville. Admiral Lord Nelson and the British fleet docked here for a while, making the port of this country a main attraction for tourists. The culinary accent is fresh fish, caught in abundance off the island's shores, and the unique Antigua black pineapple.

4 5- to 6-ounce flounder fillets

2 teaspoons salt

2 teaspoons freshly ground black pepper

   Juice of 2 limes

4 teaspoons butter

4 slices bacon → *microwave slightly first*

4 ripe bananas, peeled and mashed

2 sprigs fresh parsley, finely chopped

1 Scotch bonnet pepper, seeded and finely chopped

1. Sprinkle the flounder with salt and pepper and place in a shallow pan. Pour the lime juice on top and marinate for at least 30 minutes, covered and refrigerated.

2. Preheat an outdoor grill or preheat the oven to 375°F. Tear off 4 generous strips of aluminum foil, large enough to wrap a fillet, and spread a teaspoon of butter on each.

3. Remove the fillets from the marinade. Place one strip of bacon on each sheet of foil, and spread about half of a mashed banana on top. Place a fish fillet over this and add another half of mashed banana. Sprinkle the fillets with the parsley and Scotch bonnet pepper and cover completely with foil, leaving the top loose.

4. Grill or bake the fish for 15 to 20 minutes, checking occasionally. Open the top of the foil for the last 5 minutes. Serve immediately.

Serves 4

TUNA STEAKS WITH MANGO AND FOUR-PEPPER SAUCE

Believe it or not, the mango is not native to the New World. Persian voyagers brought this treasure to East Africa, where it later made the journey to the Caribbean islands in slave and cargo ships. We have combined this earthy fruit with the vibrant color and taste of four peppers to create a delightful sauce that is perfect on grilled tuna or just about any fish. Try it on chicken or red meat too.

4 6- to 8-ounce tuna steaks
   Juice of 2 limes
½ cup mango nectar
½ cup (1 stick) butter
2 cloves garlic, minced
1 green mango, peeled, pitted, and thinly sliced
1 small white onion, thinly sliced
1 red pepper, seeded and thinly sliced
1 green pepper, seeded and thinly sliced
1 yellow pepper, seeded and thinly sliced
1½ teaspoons finely chopped Scotch bonnet pepper
2 sprigs fresh parsley, finely chopped
2 sprigs fresh coriander, finely chopped
½ teaspoon salt
½ teaspoon freshly ground black pepper

1. In a large bowl, combine the tuna steaks with the lime juice and ¼ cup of the mango nectar. Coat well, cover, and marinate in the refrigerator for at least 30 minutes.

2. In a heavy skillet, melt ¼ cup of the butter and sauté the garlic until it is crisp. Add the mango, onion slices, red, green, and yellow peppers, Scotch bonnet pepper, and remaining mango nectar. Let this simmer, stirring constantly, until it begins to thicken, about 10 minutes. Add the parsley, coriander, salt, and pepper and continue to stir. Cook for another 5 minutes, set aside, and keep warm.

3. Preheat an outdoor grill. In a small saucepan, melt the remaining ¼ cup butter and stir in the marinade from the tuna steaks. While grilling the tuna, baste liberally with this sauce. Grill for about 6 minutes on each side. You can also pan-fry the steaks: Melt the butter in a heavy skillet and add the nectar. Stir until smooth, add the steaks, and fry until tender and fully cooked.

4. Place the tuna steaks on individual serving plates and top with the mango-pepper sauce. Serve immediately.

Serves 4

Seafood

GRILLED SHARK WITH ORANGE SAUCE

Grilled fish fillets topped with fruit sauces are a perfect example of Caribbean cuisine. This recipe can also be prepared with tuna or swordfish. The secret is in the marinade.

Fish

The waters surrounding the islands in the Caribbean teem with a variety of easy-to-catch fish. Grilled, baked, fried, or poached; sauced, souped, or served plain— fish are central to every island's cuisine.

The secret to a perfect fish dish is freshness. Fish is fragile and loses its subtle flavor quickly after being caught. The best way to buy fresh fish is to search out a reputable shop that is busy and has a picky clientele. Remember that fish cooks quickly because its meat is extremely delicate. To test a fish for doneness, gently probe it with a knife or fork to see if it flakes. You should allow 10 minutes per inch of thickness for whole fish. Fillets and steaks cook more quickly.

1 cup orange marmalade

1 tablespoon prepared horseradish

1 teaspoon hot red pepper sauce

3 cloves garlic, minced

2 sprigs fresh coriander, finely chopped

Juice of 1 lime

¼ cup pineapple juice

¼ cup dark rum

½ teaspoon salt

½ teaspoon freshly ground black pepper

½ cup olive oil

4 6- to 8-ounce shark fillets

Grated lime rind, for garnish

1. In a large bowl, combine the orange marmalade, horseradish, hot sauce, garlic, and coriander. Stir in the lime juice, pineapple juice, rum, salt, and pepper. Slowly add the olive oil, stirring constantly until all the ingredients have thoroughly combined. Place the shark fillets in the sauce, cover, and refrigerate for at least 1 hour. Preheat an outdoor grill.

2. Remove the fillets from the marinade and grill for about 6 minutes on each side or until completely cooked. While grilling, brush the marinade liberally over the fish. Heat any remaining marinade and serve as a dipping sauce at the table. Before serving, garnish the fillets with grated lime rind.

Serves 4

SWORDFISH AND PINEAPPLE BROCHETTE

Pineapple is a great fruit for grilling. Its meat is firm and stands up to the heat of a hot fire. This simple recipe, which can be prepared well in advance and marinated, offers a light alternative to steak for a summertime barbecue.

1½   **pounds swordfish steaks, cubed**

1   **large pineapple, peeled, cored, and cubed**

½   **cup (1 stick) butter**

MARINADE:

½   **cup white wine vinegar**

    Juice of 1 lime

1   **small white onion, chopped**

½   **green pepper, seeded and chopped**

1   **Scotch bonnet pepper, seeded and chopped**

2   **cloves garlic**

1   **teaspoon salt**

1   **teaspoon freshly ground black pepper**

1   **teaspoon sweet paprika**

1   **teaspoon ground coriander**

1. Alternate the cubes of swordfish and pineapple on 4 wooden skewers. In a large bowl, combine the ingredients for the marinade. Lay the brochette skewers in a large shallow dish and pour the marinade over them. Cover and refrigerate for at least 1 hour.

2. Preheat an outdoor grill. Remove the brochettes from the marinade and set them aside. In a blender or food processor, puree the marinade until it is smooth. In a small saucepan, melt the butter and slowly stir in the marinade. Transfer to a bowl.

3. Brush the brochettes with the butter sauce and grill for 4 to 5 minutes on each side while liberally basting with the sauce. Serve immediately.

Serves 4

Seafood

FLYING FISH PIE *(Barbados)*

The flying fish, caught exclusively off the coast of Barbados, is so important to this island country that it is part of the national emblem. With fins that look a lot like dragonfly wings, the fish appears to fly as it leaves the water to escape larger predators. It vibrates its tailfin in the water and gathers enough speed to propel itself into the air for 100 yards or more, traveling at 30 miles per hour. Flying fish can be prepared in a variety of ways, and this recipe is one of the most interesting. You can substitute a more available fish such as halibut or swordfish for equally delicious results.

4 green onions, chopped

1 clove garlic

4 sprigs fresh parsley

2 tablespoons dried marjoram

1 teaspoon salt

1 teaspoon freshly ground black pepper

4 6- to 8-ounce flying fish fillets

Juice of 1 lime

1 pound sweet potatoes (about 2)

2 tablespoons butter

1 egg, beaten

Bread crumbs for coating fish

Oil for frying

1 large tomato, sliced

1 large white onion, thinly sliced

2 hard-cooked eggs, peeled and sliced

1 cup prepared brown gravy

1. Place the green onions, garlic, parsley, and marjoram in a food processor and process until mushy; set aside. Salt and pepper the fillets and sprinkle with the lime juice. Pat the processed mixture onto both sides of the fillets, cover, and refrigerate for at least 1 hour.

2. Peel and cube the sweet potatoes and place in a medium saucepan. Add enough water to cover and bring to a boil. Lower the heat and simmer for 25 to 30 minutes or until the potatoes are tender. Drain off the water and return the potatoes to the saucepan. Mash the potatoes until they are smooth and fluffy. Add the butter, stir well to combine, and set aside.

3. Remove the fish from the marinade. Dip each fillet in the beaten egg and coat with bread crumbs. Heat ½ inch of oil in a heavy iron skillet and fry the fish until golden brown, about 4 minutes on each side. Drain on paper towels and set aside.

4. Preheat the oven to 350°F. Grease a casserole dish and place a layer of fried fish on the bottom. Top the fish with a layer of sliced tomato, onion, and hard-cooked egg. Spoon on half of the gravy. Repeat the layers and spread the sweet potatoes evenly over the casserole. Dot with butter and a slice of tomato and onion. Bake for 30 minutes or until bubbly.

Serves 4

CODFISH STEW

odfish, called *bacalao* in Spanish, is used in a number of ways and is especially delicious in a stew. The dried fish holds up well to slow simmering. This stew is usually prepared in heavy iron pots called *calderas* and served in bowls with white rice and wedges of ripe avocado.

- ¼ cup olive oil
- 2 cloves garlic, minced
- 1 Spanish onion, finely chopped
- 1 pound dried salt cod, prepared (page 11)
- 3 sprigs fresh coriander, finely chopped
- 1 tablespoon chopped capers
- ¼ cup chopped green olives with pimientos
- 2 large potatoes, peeled and cubed
- 1 8-ounce can tomato sauce
- ½ cup water
- 1 bay leaf
- 1 tablespoon dried thyme

In a large Dutch oven, heat the olive oil. Add the garlic and onion and sauté until they become limp. Add the codfish, coriander, capers, and olives and stir for about 2 minutes. Add the potatoes, tomato sauce, water, bay leaf, and thyme. Bring to a boil, lower the heat to simmer, and cook for about 40 minutes or until the potatoes are tender. Serve with white rice.

Serves 4 to 6

Seafood

CODFISH WITH COCONUT *(Dominican Republic)*

T he milk of a coconut makes more than just a refreshing drink. It can be used to add a subtle flavor to stews, soups, and beans. For this dish, a favorite from the Dominican Republic, be sure to use only fresh coconut meat.

Dominican Republic

Not only does the Dominican Republic have outstanding Spanish cuisine, it is an island full of history. It was a stronghold in the Spanish Empire. Christopher Columbus is buried in the Cathedral of Santa Maria la Menoir, and his son was the viceroy for many years. The island was originally called Hispaniola, and today the Dominican Republic makes up two-thirds of the island; the other third is Haiti. The native people, who are mestizo, share a passion for great food, merengue music, and dancing. Every year they celebrate this heritage with a ten-day Merengue Festival when the music and dancing do not stop.

¼ cup olive oil

1 green pepper, seeded and finely chopped

1 large white onion, finely chopped

2 cloves garlic, minced

2 tomatoes, peeled and cubed

1 cup coconut cream (page 10)

2 pounds dried salt cod, prepared (page 11)

2 sprigs fresh parsley, finely chopped

2 sprigs fresh coriander, finely chopped

½ teaspoon finely chopped Scotch bonnet pepper (optional)

½ cup water

2 medium potatoes, peeled and cubed

1 cup grated coconut meat

1 teaspoon salt

1 teaspoon freshly ground black pepper

   Parsley or coriander leaves, for garnish

In a medium saucepan, heat the olive oil and sauté the green pepper, onion, and garlic until they become limp. Add the tomatoes and coconut milk and stir to combine the ingredients well. Let this cook for about 5 minutes, then add the codfish, parsley, coriander, and Scotch bonnet pepper. Stir well and add the water. Bring to a boil and add the potatoes, coconut, salt, and black pepper. Cover and simmer over moderate to low heat until the potatoes are tender, about 20 minutes. Remove the cover and let the stew simmer and thicken slightly for another 10 minutes. Serve in soup bowls with hot white rice. Garnish with chopped parsley or coriander leaves.

Serves 6

TROPICAL BARBECUE SHRIMP

Pablo created this crowd-pleasing dish, which is always a sell-out at Sugar Reef. It is a perfect blending of fresh fruit, spices, and seafood—all the wonderful ingredients characteristic of Caribbean cuisine.

3   pounds large shrimp, peeled and deveined

1   large white onion

1   large green pepper

1   orange, peeled

MARINADE:
    Juice of 4 oranges

4   cloves garlic, chopped

2   green onions, finely chopped

¼   cup Worcestershire sauce

BARBECUE SAUCE:
¼   cup vegetable oil

¼   cup brown sugar

1   white onion, chopped

1   red onion, chopped

3   cloves garlic, minced

1   orange, peeled and chopped

3   tomatoes, pureed

1   cup Pickapeppa sauce

1   cup tomato sauce

    Juice of 2 lemons

2   tablespoons ground cumin

2   tablespoons white pepper

1   tablespoon freshly ground black pepper

1   teaspoon cayenne pepper

    Hot red pepper sauce to taste

1. In a large bowl, combine the marinade ingredients and add the shrimp. Cover and refrigerate for at least 1 hour. Cut the onion, green pepper, and orange into equal-size chunks.

2. To prepare the barbecue sauce, heat the oil in a heavy saucepan and add the brown sugar. Stir constantly over moderate heat until the sugar melts and begins to carmelize. Add the onions and garlic and mix well. Stir in the orange and pureed tomatoes and allow the mixture to simmer for 10 minutes over low to moderate heat. Add the Pickapeppa sauce, tomato sauce, and lemon juice as well as the marinade from the shrimp. Continue to cook on medium heat until the sauce begins to thicken. Add the cumin, white pepper, black pepper, and cayenne pepper and simmer another 5 to 10 minutes. Add hot sauce to taste.

3. Preheat an outdoor grill. Place the shrimp on skewers, alternating with the chunks of onion, green pepper, and orange. Grill over hot coals for 10 minutes, 5 minutes per side, while liberally basting with the barbecue sauce. Serve immediately and place extra sauce on the table for dipping.

Serves 8

Seafood

SHRIMP AND CONCH BROCHETTE

C onch has a flavor much like that of a clam but is sweeter and more delicate. Teamed with shrimp and lightly marinated, it makes an impressive entree. If you don't have access to conch meat, try making a brochette of shrimp and sea scallops.

St. Kitt

Originally named St. Christopher for Columbus's patron saint, this island is famous for its beauty, climate, and elegant way of life. In plantation days sugar was king, and St. Kitt was a very prosperous place. The royalty of Europe vacationed here long before the discovery of America. The island was formed by a volcanic eruption, and many of the beaches on St. Kitt have black volcanic sand, which contrasts sharply with the beautiful turquoise sea. The highlight of the year is Carnival, which is celebrated from December 26 to January 2. One can sample the finest of West Indian cuisine and, of course, several rum punches!

½   pound large shrimp, peeled and deveined

½   pound prepared conch meat (page 11), cubed

½   cup (1 stick) butter

Juice of 2 lemons

MARINADE:

½   cup chicken stock

½   cup white wine vinegar

Juice of 1 lime

1   white onion, finely chopped

1   green pepper, seeded and finely chopped

1   Scotch bonnet pepper, seeded and finely chopped

3   green onions, finely chopped

1   teaspoon salt

1   teaspoon freshly ground black pepper

1   teaspoon sweet paprika

1   teaspoon ground coriander

1. Alternate the shrimp and conch on 6 wooden or metal skewers. In a large bowl, combine the ingredients for the marinade. Place the brochette skewers in a large shallow dish and pour the marinade over them. Cover and refrigerate for at least 2 hours.

2. Preheat an outdoor grill. Remove the brochettes from the marinade and set them aside. Pour the marinade through a strainer, discarding the liquid, and puree the vegetables in a blender or food processor. In a small saucepan, melt the butter and slowly stir in the lemon juice. Add the pureed vegetables and stir to blend well.

3. Brush the brochettes with the butter sauce and grill for about 6 minutes on each side, while liberally basting with sauce. Serve while hot.

Serves 6

SHRIMP STEW

Although the Spanish name for this dish translates as shrimp soup, we call our version a stew because of its consistency. It is packed with olives, peppers, onion, shrimp, and fresh herbs and served in bowls with white rice.

¼ cup olive oil

4 cloves garlic, minced

1 red onion, finely chopped

1 teaspoon chopped jalapeño pepper

½ cup green olives with pimientos

4 sprigs fresh coriander, finely chopped

1 8-ounce can tomato sauce

½ cup water

3 tomatoes, peeled and cubed

2 bay leaves

2 teaspoons salt

2 teaspoons freshly ground black pepper

2 pounds medium shrimp, peeled and deveined

Chopped coriander, for garnish

1. In a heavy Dutch oven, heat the olive oil and sauté the garlic, onion, and jalapeño pepper until they are limp. Add the olives, coriander, tomato sauce, water, tomatoes, bay leaves, salt, and black pepper and stir well to combine. Bring the mixture to a full boil, lower the heat, and simmer, covered, for 20 to 30 minutes, stirring occasionally.

2. Add the shrimp and stir well. Simmer, uncovered, for about 15 minutes or until the shrimp are fully cooked. Remove the bay leaves and serve with white rice in individual soup bowls. Garnish with chopped coriander.

Serves 6

Seafood

SHRIMP ETOUFFÉE

Creole cooking blends the techniques of France, Africa, Spain, and the Indians of the islands. This dish, whose name means "smothered," begins with a roux that is made by nearly burning flour in oil. It forms the basis of a sauce of tomatoes, herbs, peppers, and vegetables, which is used to smother shrimp over a bed of white rice.

1 cup ketchup

¼ cup prepared horseradish

1 cup Worcestershire sauce

¼ cup Tabasco sauce

2 cups vegetable oil

2 cups flour

1 large white onion, finely chopped

2 bunches green onions, finely chopped

½ bunch fresh parsley, finely chopped

½ stalk celery, finely chopped

3 cloves garlic, minced

2 green peppers, seeded and finely chopped

1 teaspoon sweet paprika

1 teaspoon dried thyme

1 teaspoon dried basil

1 teaspoon salt

1 teaspoon cayenne pepper

1 teaspoon freshly ground black pepper

2 cups (or less) fish stock

1 cup (2 sticks) unsalted butter

3 pounds large shrimp, peeled and deveined

8 cups cooked white rice

Chopped parsley and green onion, for garnish

1. In a small bowl, combine the ketchup, horseradish, Worcestershire sauce, and Tabasco sauce. Stir well to combine and briefly set aside.

2. In a large heavy skillet, heat the oil until very hot and stir in the flour. Stir constantly to prevent lumps until a smooth consistency is reached. Cook the roux until it is reddish brown, almost burned, then stir in the white onion, green onions, parsley, celery, garlic, green peppers, paprika, thyme, basil, salt, cayenne pepper, and black pepper. Sauté these ingredients for about 5 minutes, then add the ketchup mixture and simmer for another 5 minutes, stirring constantly. Beginning with 1 cup, add up to 2 cups of the fish stock. The sauce should be somewhat thick, not too soupy. Let this simmer, uncovered, for 10 to 15 minutes, stirring occasionally to prevent the sauce from sticking to the bottom of the skillet. Turn off the heat and cover the pan to keep the sauce warm.

3. In a separate skillet, melt part of the butter and add the shrimp. Working in batches, sauté the shrimp for about 5 minutes or until they are fully cooked. Keep warm.

4. Spoon the rice onto individual serving plates and top with about 6 of the sautéed shrimp. Smother the shrimp with the roux sauce and garnish with chopped parsley and green onion.

Serves 8 to 12

CURRIED SHRIMP AND COCONUT *(Jamaica)*

Jamaicans love curry and are masters at creating curry sauces. This is a simple one that combines curry, coconut, and peppers. It is lightly sautéed to blend the various flavors and to cook the shrimp to perfection.

1   cup white wine

1   cup chicken stock

¼   cup curry powder

1   tablespoon salt

1   tablespoon freshly ground black pepper

3   green peppers, seeded and thinly sliced

3   carrots, peeled and thinly sliced

1   cup coconut cream (page 10)

1   cup unsweetened shredded coconut

24   large shrimp, peeled and deveined

2   teaspoons cornstarch stirred into 2 tablespoons water

Chopped green onions, for garnish

In a large saucepan or skillet, heat the wine and chicken stock until it begins to boil. Lower the heat and add the curry powder, salt, and pepper. Simmer, stirring well, for about 3 minutes. Add the green peppers and carrots and simmer for 5 minutes, stirring occasionally. Add the coconut cream, ½ cup of the shredded coconut, and the shrimp and continue to stir. Simmer until the shrimp are pink and fully cooked and the vegetables are tender. Add enough cornstarch to thicken the sauce and stir well. Serve with Calabaza Pumpkin Rice (page 152) and garnish with the remaining shredded coconut and the chopped green onions.

Serves 4

Seafood

BUBBA LOU'S CRAB CAKES

Our friend Bubba Lou lives on a sailboat and calls the Caribbean home. He is a superb cook, despite the limitations of the boat's galley. Making the most of the bountiful supply of fresh tropical ingredients and keeping his preparations simple are the secrets to his success. These crab cakes can be served as a main course or an appetizer but in either case it is essential that they be served with Bubba Lou's special sauce.

6 medium shrimp, peeled and deveined

2 Scotch bonnet peppers, seeded and roasted

4 cloves garlic

2 tablespoons buttermilk

2 pounds fresh white and dark crabmeat, picked over to remove bits of cartilage

2 tomatoes, peeled, seeded, and finely chopped

½ teaspoon salt

½ teaspoon freshly ground black pepper

1 cup bread crumbs

Oil for frying

Lemon wedges, for garnish

Lime wedges, for garnish

Chopped fresh parsley, for garnish

1. Place the shrimp, Scotch bonnet peppers, garlic, and buttermilk in a food processor and process to make a paste. Transfer to a large bowl and add the crabmeat, tomatoes, salt, pepper, and bread crumbs. Stir the ingredients to combine well. Using about ½ cup of the crabmeat mixture at a time, make flat round cakes. There should be enough mix to make about 16 cakes.

2. Heat the oil in a deep fryer or heavy iron skillet to 350°F. Fry the crab cakes for about 3 minutes per side or until they are golden brown. Drain on paper towels. Arrange 2 cakes on each serving plate and garnish with lemon and lime wedges. Sprinkle with chopped fresh parsley and serve with Bubba's Tomato Butter (page 193).

Serves 8

DEVILED CRABS

No, little red devils did not create this recipe, but you will feel like one after you have a few of these tasty crabs. We specify fresh crabmeat because it has more flavor, but the canned variety will also work well.

3 tablespoons butter

3 tablespoons flour

1 cup milk

½ cup heavy cream

2 egg yolks, lightly beaten

1 pound fresh white crabmeat, shredded and drained well

2 tablespoons dry sherry

½ teaspoon finely chopped Scotch bonnet pepper

1 teaspoon salt

1 teaspoon freshly ground black pepper

Dash ground cinnamon

1 tablespoon chopped fresh parsley

6 teaspoons butter

6 tablespoons bread crumbs

Lime slices, for garnish

1. In a large saucepan, melt the butter over low heat and slowly stir in the flour until all the lumps are smoothed out. Add the milk and cream and stir constantly until the mixture begins to thicken. Stir a spoonful into the egg yolks to warm them, then add the egg yolks to the cream sauce, stirring constantly. Pick over the crabmeat to remove bits of cartilage and add to the saucepan, along with the sherry, Scotch bonnet pepper, salt, black pepper, cinnamon, and parsley. Simmer the ingredients, stirring well, for about 5 minutes. Preheat the oven to broil.

2. Remove the saucepan from the stove and divide the crabmeat mixture among 6 ramekins. Top each with a teaspoon of butter and sprinkle with a tablespoon of bread crumbs. Place the ramekins under the broiler until the bread crumbs are golden brown and the crabmeat is bubbly. Garnish each one with a slice of lime and serve immediately.

Serves 6

Seafood

CRAB PILAU

This West Indian dish was heavily influenced by the East Indians who now call the Caribbean home. It combines fresh crabmeat, curry, peppers, and coconut.

1   pound fresh white and dark crabmeat

1   teaspoon salt

1   teaspoon freshly ground black pepper

    Juice of 1 lime

½   cup (1 stick) butter

1   large white onion, finely chopped

2   cloves garlic, minced

1   Scotch bonnet pepper, seeded and finely chopped

2   tablespoons curry powder

1   tomato, cubed

1¾ cups long-grain rice

3½ cups coconut cream (page 10)

1. Pick over the crabmeat to remove any bits of cartilage and place in a medium bowl. Add the salt, pepper, and lime juice and stir to mix well. Cover and refrigerate for at least 1 hour.

2. In a large Dutch oven, melt the butter and sauté the onion, garlic, and Scotch bonnet pepper until they become limp, stirring constantly. Add the curry powder and continue to stir for about 3 minutes. Add the tomato, combine well with the other ingredients, and sauté for 3 minutes more, stirring occasionally. Add the rice and continue to stir, making sure that the rice grains get covered. Mix in the coconut cream, lower the heat, and cover the Dutch oven.

3. Simmer the rice for about 15 minutes or until it is almost done. Add the crabmeat with its marinade and stir well to combine. Cover the Dutch oven and simmer until all the liquids have been absorbed, about 5 minutes longer. Serve, if you like, with Mango Chutney (page 191).

Serves 6

CALALOU *(Guadeloupe)*

Okra makes this recipe for Calalou different from the Trinidad version (page 47). It's a delicious rendition that came to us through Madame Prudence Marcelin of Guadeloupe.

2   to 3 pounds fresh spinach, stems removed, chopped

2   pounds fresh kale, stems removed, chopped

¼   cup vegetable oil

½   cup chopped white onion

1   cup chopped green onion (including green)

1   cup chopped garlic (about 2 bulbs)

¼   cubed salt pork (or smoked ham or pig's tail)

1   pound fresh white and dark crabmeat

1½ cups lime juice

1   pound okra, stem ends removed, chopped

2   Scotch bonnet peppers, seeded and finely chopped

1   tablespoon salt

1   tablespoon freshly ground black pepper

4   cups water

Bouquet garni (1 green onion, 2 sprigs fresh thyme, 2 sprigs fresh parsley)

Lime slices, for garnish

Chopped fresh parsley, for garnish

1. Thoroughly rinse the spinach and kale in cold water. Place in a large stockpot and add water to cover. Bring to a boil, lower the heat, and simmer, covered, until the vegetables are soft and limp, about 15 minutes.

2. In a large saucepan, heat the oil over medium heat and sauté the white onion, green onions, garlic, and salt pork until lightly brown. Set aside briefly.

3. Pick over the crabmeat to remove any bits of cartilage. Place in a colander and rinse in cold water. Shake off the excess water and add ½ cup of the lime juice. Toss well and again shake off the excess liquid. Add the crabmeat to the onion and salt pork mixture and stir well so that the crabmeat will absorb the flavors.

4. Remove the spinach and kale from the stove and drain off the cooking water, saving at least 1 cup. Place in a food processor and puree. Use the cooking water to keep the mixture soupy.

5. Put the pureed vegetables back into the stockpot and add the crabmeat mixture. Stir in the okra, Scotch bonnet peppers, remaining lime juice, salt, and black pepper. Add the water and bouquet garni, mix well, and bring to a boil over medium heat. Lower the heat and let the Calalou simmer for 20 minutes or until the okra has softened and thickens the broth. Serve in large soup bowls over white rice. Garnish with thin slices of lime and chopped parsley.

Seafood

Serves 10 to 12

CARIBBEAN CRABMEAT STUFFING

You can have a field day with this savory stuffing. It is great spooned into papaya shells or baked in any kind of squash. It can even be served alone, baked in a dish or placed atop a bed of fresh greens.

St. Barthelemy

Named for Christopher Columbus's baby brother, this rocky mountainous island has a total mass of just 8 square miles. It is home to many well-to-do American and French families and in the 1950s was considered the St. Tropez of the Caribbean, thanks in large part to its numerous nude beaches. St. Barts is one of the few islands in the Caribbean that is predominantly Caucasian; a small percentage of the population is descended from slaves who escaped here, as slavery never existed on this island. It is a department of Guadeloupe, and French is the official language. Restaurants on St. Barts offer some of the finest examples of French and Creole cuisine.

¼ cup (½ stick) butter

2 stalks celery, finely chopped

1 white onion, finely chopped

1 small red onion, finely chopped

1 carrot, finely chopped

1 green pepper, seeded and finely chopped

1 tomato, cubed

1 pound fresh white and dark crabmeat, picked over to remove bits of cartilage

1 tablespoon Old Bay Seasoning

½ teaspoon salt

½ teaspoon freshly ground black pepper

½ teaspoon dried thyme

½ teaspoon dried oregano

½ teaspoon white pepper

½ cup white wine

1 tablespoon dry vermouth

1 tablespoon brandy

½ cup bread crumbs

1. In a Dutch oven, melt the butter and add the celery, onions, carrot, green pepper, and tomato. Sauté for about 3 minutes, then add the crabmeat. Stir and cook for another 5 minutes.

2. Add the Old Bay Seasoning, salt, black pepper, thyme, oregano, white pepper, white wine, vermouth, and brandy. Simmer the mixture, stirring well, for about 10 minutes. Add the bread crumbs to thicken and continue to stir. Remove the stuffing from the stove and use it to stuff the vegetable of your choice. It is also excellent alone. Spoon into individual baking dishes and bake for 30 minutes at 350°F. Serve while hot.

Serves 6

GRILLED LOBSTER WITH AVOCADO MAYONNAISE

Rock lobster is the most common variety of lobster caught in the Caribbean. It is different from its North Atlantic cousin. The most noticeable difference is the lack of a large pincer claw and the long antennae and spines on its body and legs. For this recipe any kind of lobster will do.

4 live 1-pound lobsters

½ cup (1 stick) butter, melted

Juice of 2 lemons

2 cloves garlic, minced

1 teaspoon black pepper

1 teaspoon salt

1 cup Avocado Mayonnaise (page 195)

Lime or lemon wedges, for garnish

1. Fill a lobster pot or very large stockpot two-thirds full of water and bring to a rolling boil. Place 2 or 3 lobsters at a time in the pot, cover quickly, and boil, holding the lid down, for 5 minutes. Remove the lobsters and, when cool enough to handle, slice each one in half lengthwise with a large sharp knife or cleaver.

2. Preheat an outdoor grill. In a small bowl, combine the butter, lemon juice, garlic, pepper, and salt. Liberally coat each lobster half.

3. Place the lobster, meat side down, on the grill and cook for about 5 to 8 minutes. Turn onto the shell side and grill for another 2 to 3 minutes or until the meat easily pulls out of the shell.

4. Remove from the grill and serve immediately. Place 2 halves, meat side up, on each plate and top with Avocado Mayonnaise. Garnish with a fresh lime or lemon wedge.

Serves 4

Seafood

LANGOSTA EXQUISITA *(Dominican Republic)*

Our chef Pablo prepares this Dominican specialty by flash boiling and then grilling the lobster. His topping of creamy mustard sauce is a finishing touch that makes the name of this recipe perfect.

Don't Touch Me Tomato
George Symonette
Bahama Records, 1954

*Please, mister, don't
touch me tomato.
Touch me yam, me po-
tato,
For goodness sake,
don't touch me
tomato.
Touch me everything I
have got,
Touch me apple, touch
me plum too.
Here's one thing you
just can't do.
All you do is feel em,
feel em,
Ain't you tired of peel
em, peel em?
Please, mister, take my
advice,
The more you look, the
less you see.
If you just might have
your way,
Double the price you
got to pay.
All you do is squeeze
em, squeeze em.
Touch me yam, touch
me pumpkin potato,
Please, mister, don't
touch me tomato!*

6   live 1-pound lobsters
½   cup (1 stick) butter, melted
    Juice of 2 limes
2   cloves garlic, minced
1   teaspoon salt
1   teaspoon freshly ground black pepper
    Lime wedges, for garnish

SAUCE:
½   cup (1 stick) butter
1   small green pepper, seeded and finely chopped
1   small white onion, finely chopped
2   sprigs fresh parsley, finely chopped
2   sprigs fresh coriander, finely chopped
3   tablespoons flour
½   cup tomato sauce
1   12-ounce can evaporated milk
2   tablespoons Worcestershire sauce
1   tablespoon Dijon mustard
1   tablespoon hot red pepper sauce (optional)
1   teaspoon salt
1   teaspoon white pepper
4   egg yolks
⅓   cup chicken stock (optional)

1. Flash-boil the lobsters following the directions in the recipe on page 82.

2. Preheat an outdoor grill. In a small bowl, combine the butter, lime juice, garlic, salt, and pepper. Liberally cover each lobster half and set aside while you make the sauce.

3. In a medium saucepan, melt the butter and sauté the green pepper, onion, parsley, and coriander until they become limp. Slowly stir in the flour and continue to cook and stir for about 5 minutes. Add the tomato sauce and evaporated milk and mix in. Cook for a few minutes, then stir in the Worcestershire sauce, mustard, hot sauce, salt, pepper, and egg yolks. The sauce will begin to thicken to a heavy cream consistency. If you prefer a lighter sauce, you may add up to ⅓ cup chicken stock. Remove the sauce from the stove, cover, and set aside.

4. Place the lobster, meat side down, on the grill and cook for about 5 minutes. Turn onto the shell side and brush the meat with the butter-lime mixture. Grill until the meat easily pulls out of the shell.

5. Remove and place 2 halves on individual serving plates. Reheat the creamy mustard sauce and spoon over the lobster. Garnish with lime wedges and chopped coriander.

Serves 6

BAKED LOBSTER

Since lobster is abundant along the shores of the Caribbean, the chefs there have come up with lots of ideas and techniques for preparing it. In this recipe the lobster is baked in a light butter, onion, and pepper sauce. It is great as a main course but can be served in small portions as an appetizer.

2 **pounds fresh lobster meat, cubed**

Juice of 1 lime

1 **teaspoon salt**

1 **teaspoon freshly ground black pepper**

½ **cup (1 stick) unsalted butter**

2 **cloves garlic, minced**

1 **Scotch bonnet pepper, seeded and finely chopped (optional)**

2 **white onions, finely chopped**

1 **red pepper, seeded and finely chopped**

¼ **cup bread crumbs**

3 **teaspoons Pickapeppa sauce (or 1½ teaspoons mango chutney and 1½ teaspoons Worcestershire sauce)**

Lobster claws, for garnish

1. Place the lobster meat in a large bowl and add the lime juice, salt, and pepper. Stir well to coat and let the lobster marinate at room temperature for 20 minutes.

2. In a heavy iron skillet, melt half of the butter and sauté the garlic, Scotch bonnet pepper, onions, and red pepper until they are limp. Add 2 tablespoons of the bread crumbs and sauté until they turn golden brown, about 3 minutes. Add the lobster, marinade, remaining butter, and Pickapeppa sauce. Stir the ingredients well and let them simmer until the lobster begins to cook on the outer edges, for 2 to 3 minutes. Preheat the oven to 350°F.

3. Remove the skillet from the stove and transfer its contents to a baking dish. Top the lobster with the remaining bread crumbs and place 2 lobster claws on top. Bake for 25 to 30 minutes or until the mixture is bubbly and the bread crumbs are golden brown.

Serves 4

Seafood

LOBSTER SALAD *(Barbados)*

In the Caribbean, lobster is offered in an array of styles to eager diners. This excellent luncheon salad offers the advantage of advance preparation. Although it is best made with fresh lobster, the frozen variety is an agreeable substitute.

2 pounds fresh lobster meat, cubed

4 green onions, finely chopped

2 sprigs fresh parsley, finely chopped

3 hard-cooked eggs, mashed

4 stalks celery, finely chopped

¼ cup chopped red pepper

¼ cup chopped green pepper

1 tablespoon lime juice

1 teaspoon salt

1 teaspoon freshly ground black pepper

½ cup mayonnaise

Lettuce, for garnish

Lime wedges, for garnish

In a large bowl, combine the lobster, green onions, parsley, eggs, celery, red pepper, green pepper, lime juice, salt, and black pepper. Lightly toss the ingredients until thoroughly mixed. Add the mayonnaise and stir until all the ingredients are coated. Cover the bowl and refrigerate until the salad is completely chilled, about 2 hours. Serve over a bed of fresh lettuce and garnish with fresh lime wedges.

Serves 4

Chicken

BAKED CHICKEN WITH LIME AND GINGER

C hicken is popular on the islands but not native to the region. These familiar birds originated in the jungles of Southeast Asia and made their way to the Caribbean along with traders on slave ships from around the world. This dish combines ginger and lime to create a great Sunday dinner.

3   **tablespoons grated fresh ginger**

2   **cloves garlic, minced**

1   **small white onion, finely chopped**

½   **cup lime juice**

1   **4- to 5-pound chicken, giblets removed**

2   **tablespoons butter**

1   **teaspoon salt**

1   **teaspoon freshly ground black pepper**

3   **tablespoons mango chutney, chopped**

1   **teaspoon cornstarch stirred into 1 tablespoon water**

1. Combine the ginger, garlic, onion, and lime juice to make a paste. Rub the bird inside and out with the mixture. Place in a large bowl, cover, and refrigerate for at least 1 hour.

2. Preheat the oven to 350°F. Remove the chicken from its bowl and briefly set aside. In a small saucepan, melt the butter and add the juices from the chicken, stirring well. Sprinkle salt and pepper on the chicken, set in a roasting pan, and pour the butter mixture over the bird. Bake for 1 to 1½ hours.

3. Remove the chicken from the roasting pan and drain the drippings into a small saucepan. Heat over moderate heat, stir in the chutney, and simmer for about 5 minutes. Add the cornstarch to thicken and serve hot as a gravy.

Serves 4

Chicken

POULET FRICASSÉ *(Guadeloupe)*

This recipe came to us through Madame Prudence Marcelin of Guadeloupe. When we asked the Guadeloupe tourist office to arrange for a chef to visit our New York kitchen, Mme Marcelin was their instant choice. A dynamic personality and talented cook, she prepared the state dinner when President Jimmy Carter and President Valéry Giscard d'Estaing of France visited the island to have a summit meeting.

Guadeloupe

True Caribbean cuisine can be very hard to find on many islands. Most restaurants and hotels tend to cater to Anglo tastes, and most island people prefer to eat at home. As a result, many tourists return from a Caribbean vacation without any idea of the local cuisine. The exception is the island of Guadeloupe, where food is a way of life. Some of the finest restaurants in the West Indies are nestled along its shores.

¾ to 1 cup lime juice

1 tablespoon freshly ground black pepper

1 tablespoon salt

½ cup green onions, chopped

2 sprigs fresh parsley, finely chopped

2 to 3 sprigs fresh thyme, finely chopped

1 cup chopped garlic (about 2 heads)

2 4- to 5-pound chickens, cut into serving pieces

2 beefsteak or other large tomatoes

¼ cup pitted green olives

¼ cup capers, drained

½ cup vegetable oil

1 white onion, finely chopped

Water

Bouquet garni (1 green onion, 2 sprigs fresh thyme, 2 sprigs fresh parsley)

1 6-ounce can tomato paste

½ cup dry white wine

Avocado slices, for garnish

1. In a large saucepan, mix together the lime juice, pepper, salt, green onions, parsley, thyme, and garlic. Stir well and add the chicken pieces. Let the chicken marinate in the mixture for at least 30 minutes, covered and refrigerated.

2. In a food processor, puree the tomatoes, olives, and capers. Set aside for later use.

3. Heat the oil in a Dutch oven, add the onion, and sauté until limp and golden. Add the chicken pieces and set the marinade aside. Turn the pieces and sauté until they begin to turn white. At this point add the marinade, pureed tomatoes, and enough water to cover all the chicken. Add the bouquet garni and simmer over medium heat for 20 minutes, stirring occasionally.

4. Add the tomato paste, white wine, and ¾ cup water. Stir well and cover. Simmer on low to medium heat for 2 hours or until the chicken easily separates from the bone. Discard the bouquet garni. Garnish with avocado slices and serve with white rice.

Serves 6 to 8

POULET BONNE FEMME

This Creole dish made its way to New Orleans via Haitian slaves. In fact, many African and Indian dishes became traditional in white families because African slaves once worked in their kitchens.

½ teaspoon salt

1 teaspoon freshly ground black pepper

2 cups flour

2 4- to 5-pound chickens, cut into serving pieces

6 strips bacon, cut into ¼-inch strips

1 white onion, chopped

1 bulb (whole head) garlic, minced

3 cups water

2 sprigs fresh parsley, finely chopped

3 potatoes, peeled and diced

1. Mix the salt and pepper with the flour and roll each piece of chicken in it, shaking off the excess.

2. In a large Dutch oven over medium heat, fry the bacon slices until they begin to render fat, then remove and discard. Add the onion and garlic and sauté until limp. Turn up the heat, add the chicken pieces, and brown for 10 to 15 minutes, turning frequently.

3. Add the water, parsley, and potatoes and bring the water to a boil. Lower the heat to a simmer, cover, and cook for 30 minutes, stirring occasionally, until the potatoes are tender. If necessary, add more water. When cooked the chicken and potatoes should be fairly dry. Add more salt and pepper if needed.

Serves 6 to 8

Chicken

BAKED CHICKEN WITH POTATOES *(Puerto Rico)*

 Garlic, lime, and oregano are three favorite ingredients in Puerto Rican cooking, and this dish uses them all. It's usually prepared for large family gatherings on Sundays, but we've cut the recipe down to a more manageable size.

Puerto Rico

It may be an unincorporated United States territory, but Puerto Rico's emotional ties are purely Latin. Spanish is the official language, not English. The island was discovered by Christopher Columbus and given a name that means "rich port." The first governor was Ponce de Leon, a famous explorer in his own right.

Festivals and holidays are a way of life on Puerto Rico and feature some of the finest examples of Spanish cuisine: black bean soup, chicharrone de pollo, *fried plantains,* flan, and bacaloa. Rum *is produced here and the island claims the* piña colada *as its own invention. In fact, most tours include a trip to pineapple plantations and rum distilleries.*

MARINADE:

- 2 cloves garlic, minced
- 2 teaspoons salt
- 2 teaspoons dried oregano
- 1½ teaspoons freshly ground black pepper
- 1 tablespoon olive oil
  Juice of 1 lime

- 1 3- to 4-pound chicken, cut into serving pieces
- ½ cup (1 stick) butter, melted
- 2 pounds new potatoes, boiled, peeled, and sliced
- 1 teaspoon salt
- 1 teaspoon freshly ground black pepper

1. In a large bowl, stir all the marinade ingredients together to form a paste. Liberally rub it on the chicken pieces, cover, and marinate for at least 1 hour in the refrigerator.

2. Preheat the oven to 350°F. Transfer the chicken with its marinade to a casserole or baking dish and rub each piece with butter. Bake for 1 hour, uncovered, basting occasionally.

3. Remove the chicken from the oven, arrange the potato slices around the dish, and sprinkle with salt and pepper. Return to the oven and continue to bake for another 30 minutes, basting occasionally. Serve immediately.

Serves 4

91

FOWL DOWN IN RICE

This is chicken prepared to perfection. The unusual name comes from placing the chicken in a cozy bed of piping hot white rice. For a contrast in tastes, try serving it with a fresh tropical fruit salad.

1 3- to 4-pound chicken, cut into serving pieces

1 tablespoon salt

1 tablespoon freshly ground black pepper

Juice of 2 limes

2¼ cups chicken stock

4 cups water

2 sprigs fresh thyme

2 green onions, finely chopped

2 sprigs fresh parsley, finely chopped

3 whole cloves

¼ cup (½ stick) butter

1 large white onion, finely chopped

1 teaspoon dry mustard

2 tomatoes, peeled and cubed

4 cups long-grain rice

1. Rub the chicken pieces with 2 teaspoons each of the salt and pepper. Place the chicken in a large bowl and sprinkle with the lime juice. Cover the bowl and refrigerate for at least 1 hour.

2. In a Dutch oven, bring 2 cups of the chicken stock and the water, thyme, green onions, parsley, and cloves to a boil. Add the chicken, lower the heat, and simmer, uncovered, for 40 minutes.

3. In a medium saucepan, melt the butter and sauté the onion until limp. Add the mustard, tomatoes, remaining chicken stock, and remaining salt and pepper. Stir occasionally and let it simmer for about 10 minutes. Transfer to the Dutch oven, and stir in the rice. Lower the heat, cover, and simmer until the rice is tender and all of the liquid has been absorbed, about 30 minutes.

Serves 4

Chicken

POULET COLOMBO

Curry spices were introduced to the Caribbean by East Indians who were brought in as indentured servants and slaves. The French Creoles on Guadeloupe and Martinique incorporated curry into their cooking with wondrous results, as this recipe attests.

½   cup white wine vinegar

Juice of 3 limes

2   4- to 5-pound chickens, cut into serving pieces

1   teaspoon salt

1   teaspoon freshly ground black pepper

¼   cup annatto oil or vegetable oil

4   cloves garlic, minced

¼   cup curry powder

½   cup water

2   cups chicken stock

Bouquet garni (1 green onion, 1 sprig fresh parsley, 1 sprig fresh thyme, 1 bay leaf)

5   new potatoes, peeled and cubed

3   carrots, sliced

1. In a large bowl, combine the vinegar and lime juice. Rub the chicken pieces with salt and pepper and place in the vinegar and lime. Cover and refrigerate for at least 1 hour.

2. In a large Dutch oven, heat the annatto oil and sauté the garlic until crisp. Remove the chicken from the marinade, setting aside ¼ cup for later use. Add the chicken to the Dutch oven and brown for 15 to 20 minutes, turning often.

3. In a small saucepan, combine the curry powder, reserved marinade, and water. Bring to a boil over medium heat, lower the heat, and simmer for 10 to 15 minutes, stirring occasionally.

4. When the chicken has browned, add the curry sauce to the Dutch oven and stir well. Let it begin to boil, then add the chicken stock, bouquet garni, potatoes, and carrots. Return to a boil, lower the heat, and simmer for approximately 1 hour or until the potatoes and carrots are tender and the chicken pulls easily from the bone. Add more water if necessary while cooking. Remove the bouquet garni and serve with hot white rice.

Serves 6

POLLO AL JEREZ *(Dominican Republic)*

Another version of Caribbean-style stewed chicken, this hearty dish comes to us from the Dominican Republic. Sherry adds a flavorful note to the traditional combination of chicken and vegetables.

2 tablespoons olive oil

1 3½-pound chicken, cut into serving pieces

2 cloves garlic, minced

2 stalks celery, finely chopped

2 carrots, sliced

2 beefsteak tomatoes, diced

1 bay leaf

1 teaspoon salt

1 teaspoon freshly ground black pepper

¾ cup dry sherry

2 cups water

5 new potatoes, diced

2 tablespoons chopped parsley

In a Dutch oven, heat the olive oil over moderate heat and add the chicken pieces and garlic. Brown for about 10 minutes, turning occasionally to prevent sticking. Add the celery, carrots, tomatoes, bay leaf, salt, pepper, sherry, and water and stir well. Bring the liquid to a boil, then add the potatoes. Cover the Dutch oven, lower the heat, and simmer for 20 minutes or until the potatoes are tender. Add the chopped parsley and serve over white rice.

Serves 4

Chicken

CHICKEN PEPPERPOT *(Guyana)*

A true pepperpot is prepared in a large kettle. In some families, the same pepperpot will stew for years, kept going by the continual addition of leftover ingredients from other meals. Scraps of meat, fish, vegetables, and spices create a stew that never tastes the same. The pepperpot is most common on Guyana, where it originated during plantation days. Slaves rarely got meat and perhaps stretched its flavor in a dish like this one.

MARINADE:

½ teaspoon salt

1 teaspoon freshly ground black pepper

1 teaspoon dried thyme

½ teaspoon cayenne pepper

½ teaspoon ground turmeric

Juice of 1 lime

Juice of 1 lemon

1 3- to 4-pound chicken, cut into serving pieces

½ cup (1 stick) butter

1 white onion, finely chopped

1 red onion, finely chopped

1 green pepper, seeded and finely chopped

1 Scotch bonnet pepper, seeded and finely chopped

1 cup dry white wine

2 tablespoons sweet vermouth

2 cups chicken stock

1 white turnip, peeled and cubed

1 sweet potato, peeled and cubed

6 small new potatoes, peeled and halved

4 carrots, sliced

1 sprig fresh thyme

1. In a large bowl, combine the salt, black pepper, thyme, cayenne pepper, and turmeric. Add the lime and lemon juices and stir well to make a paste. Rub the paste over each chicken piece, cover, and marinate in the refrigerator for at least 1 hour.

2. In a large Dutch oven, melt the butter over medium heat and sauté the onions, green pepper, and Scotch bonnet pepper until they are tender. Add the chicken pieces to the Dutch oven, setting aside the marinade, and brown the chicken on all sides, about 15 to 20 minutes.

3. Stir in the marinade, wine, vermouth, and chicken stock and bring to a boil, then add the turnip, potatoes, carrots, and thyme. Lower the heat and simmer, covered, for about 1 hour, stirring occasionally. The chicken should easily pull from the bone. If the vegetables are not tender, add more chicken stock and cook on low. Serve with white rice.

Serves 4 to 6

CHICHARRONE DE POLLO *(Puerto Rico)*

Nobody prepares fried chicken as well as the Puerto Ricans. Their precise blending of spices and quick deep frying produces mouth-watering morsels of chicken—crispy and flavorful on the outside, moist and tender on the inside. The chicken, hacked into bite-size pieces, is sold by street vendors throughout Puerto Rico.

MARINADE:

- 1 **bulb (whole head) garlic, separated into cloves and minced**
- 2 **teaspoons salt**
- 2 **tablespoons garlic powder**
- 1 **tablespoon onion powder**
- 1 **tablespoon freshly ground black pepper**
- 1 **tablespoon dried oregano**
- 2 **tablespoons sweet paprika**
- 2 **tablespoons ground coriander**
- 1 **tablespoon ground annatto seed (optional)**
- ½ **cup olive oil**
- ¼ **cup white vinegar**
- ½ **cup chicken stock**
- ¾ **cup lime juice**

- 1 **3- to 4-pound chicken, cut into serving pieces**

  Oil for deep frying

1. In a blender or food processor, puree all the ingredients for the marinade to make a thin paste. Pour the marinade over the chicken, cover, and refrigerate for at least 2 hours or preferably overnight.

2. Preheat the oven to 400°F. Place the chicken with the marinade in a lightly greased 9 × 13-inch baking pan and bake, uncovered, for 30 to 40 minutes. Turn and baste the chicken after 15 minutes.

3. In a deep fryer or large saucepan, heat the oil to 350°F. Remove the chicken from the oven and deep-fry each piece for about 3 minutes or until golden brown. Serve with white rice and black beans.

Serves 4

Chicken

BAJAN CHICKEN *(Barbados)*

T he secret to this dish is the expert blending of "Bajan" seasonings. The chicken is packed with tiny pockets of spice, lightly floured, and deep fried, so that each bite is crunchy and full of flavor.

Barbados

Barbados is positioned 1,200 miles from Miami, 270 miles from the coast of Venezuela, and 3,000 miles from its nearest neighbor to the east, Dakar, Africa, where Bajans say they can see the red dust of the Sahara Desert on a clear day. It is named after the bearded fig trees Columbus spotted along the shoreline. Each year at the end of sugar cane harvest, Bajans celebrate with a month-long festival called Crop Over, which involves special food, calypso music, and dancing in the streets. The food is very West Indian, and the specialty is fried flying fish. Barbados is one of the largest rum-producing countries, and the best rum punches can be found there (see page 199).

MARINADE:

- 5   green onions, chopped
- 2   white onions, chopped
- 1   green pepper, seeded and chopped
- 1   Scotch bonnet pepper, seeded and chopped
- 3   cloves garlic
- 1   tablespoon dried thyme
  Juice of 2 limes
- 1   teaspoon salt
- 1   teaspoon freshly ground black pepper

- 4   6- to 8-ounce chicken breasts, trimmed of fat
- 1   tablespoon dried rosemary
- 1   tablespoon dried sage
- ½   teaspoon dried thyme
- ½   teaspoon dried marjoram
- 1   teaspoon salt
- ½   teaspoon freshly ground black pepper
- ¼   cup (½ stick) butter, melted

1. Place all the marinade ingredients in a food processor or blender and process until the vegetables are finely chopped, about 15 seconds. Rub the marinade thoroughly over the chicken breasts, place them in a large bowl, and cover. Marinate the chicken in the refrigerator for at least 1 hour or, if possible, overnight.

2. Preheat the oven to 375°F. In a small mixing bowl, combine the rosemary, sage, thyme, marjoram, salt, and black pepper with the melted butter. Remove the chicken and add the butter to the leftover marinade. Stir well to blend completely.

3. With a sharp knife, make several shallow incisions in each chicken breast. Fill the cuts with as much of the butter paste as possible and rub any leftover paste over the outsides. Place the chicken in a 9 × 13-inch baking pan and bake for 30 minutes, turning the pieces after 15 minutes and basting with cooking juices.

4. At Sugar Reef we finish the chicken on our grill for 3 to 4 minutes per side. This enhances the flavors but is not a necessary step. If you prefer, you can bake the chicken completely, but lower the oven temperature to 350°F and increase the baking time to 45 minutes.

Serves 4

CHICKEN MONTEGO BAY *(Jamaica)*

Our chef says this dish reminds him of Montego Bay in Jamaica. It wonderfully blends eight spices and includes a variety of fresh vegetables.

1 tablespoon dried thyme

1 tablespoon salt

1 tablespoon freshly ground black pepper

1 tablespoon ground cumin

2 tablespoons dried oregano

2 tablespoons dried basil

2 tablespoons sweet paprika

2 tablespoons ground coriander

1 tablespoon ground annato seed (optional)

½ cup flour

4 6- to 8-ounce chicken breasts, skin removed

2 egg whites, lightly beaten

¼ cup olive oil

1 cup chopped okra

1 cup chopped plum tomatoes

½ cup chopped green pepper

¾ cup finely chopped white onion

½ cup chopped green onions (including green)

4 sprigs coriander, chopped

½ cup white wine

2 tablespoons dry vermouth

1. In a shallow bowl, combine the thyme, salt, pepper, cumin, oregano, basil, paprika, coriander, annato seed, and flour. Dip the chicken breasts in the egg white, shake off any excess, and roll in the flour mixture.

2. Heat the olive oil in a heavy skillet. When hot, add the chicken breasts and brown on both sides for about 5 to 8 minutes. Drain the breasts on paper towels and set aside, keeping the skillet and oil hot.

3. Sauté the okra, tomatoes, green pepper, onion, green onions, and coriander until limp, stirring well. Add the wine and vermouth and bring to a boil. Lower the heat, cover, and simmer for 15 to 20 minutes.

4. Preheat the oven to 350°F. Place the chicken breasts side by side in a 9 × 13-inch baking pan. Spoon the sautéed vegetables over the chicken and bake for 40 to 45 minutes. Served with white rice and crusty French bread.

Serves 4

Chicken

"JERK" CHICKEN SUGAR REEF STYLE

Jerk Chicken is the pride of Jamaica and is the most requested dish on the Sugar Reef menu. When prepared properly, it is a stunning, mouth-watering dish that is hard to forget. This recipe is not as hot as you would find in Jamaica. For that authentic flavor, double the quantity of dry spices.

"Jerk"

This method of cooking pork and chicken dates back to the Carib-Arawak Indians who inhabited Jamaica. After capturing an animal and thoroughly cleaning and gutting it, the Indians placed it in a deep pit lined with stones and covered with green wood, which, when burned, would smoke heavily and add to the flavor. But first the carcass was "jerked" with a sharp object to make holes, which were stuffed with a variety of spices. The holes also allowed heat to escape without loss of moisture. The results were superb. The meat was not only wonderfully spiced but moist and tender.

1 tablespoon ground allspice

1 tablespoon dried thyme

1½ teaspoons cayenne pepper

1½ teaspoons freshly ground black pepper

1½ teaspoons ground sage

¾ teaspoon ground nutmeg

¾ teaspoon ground cinnamon

2 tablespoons salt

2 tablespoons garlic powder

1 tablespoon sugar

¼ cup olive oil

¼ cup soy sauce

¾ cup white vinegar

½ cup orange juice

Juice of 1 lime

1 Scotch bonnet pepper, seeded and finely chopped

1 cup chopped white onion

3 green onions, finely chopped

4 6- to 8-ounce chicken breasts, trimmed of fat

1. In a large bowl, combine the allspice, thyme, cayenne pepper, black pepper, sage, nutmeg, cinnamon, salt, garlic powder, and sugar. With a wire whisk, slowly add the olive oil, soy sauce, vinegar, orange juice, and lime juice. Add the Scotch bonnet pepper, onion, and green onions and mix well. Add the chicken breasts, cover, and marinate for at least 1 hour, longer if possible.

2. Preheat an outdoor grill. Remove the breasts from the marinade and grill for 6 minutes on each side or until fully cooked. While grilling, baste with the marinade. Heat the leftover marinade and serve on the side for dipping.

Serves 4

SUGAR REEF CITRUS CHICKEN

Once familiar with the ingredients that make Caribbean cuisine special, you'll find it easy to be creative. This Sugar Reef original was tested by the harshest critics, our customers, and got a thumbs up.

1 8-ounce jar orange marmalade

½ cup finely chopped white onion

2 tablespoons Pickapeppa sauce

½ cup (1 stick) butter, softened

1 cup grated Gruyère cheese

4 5-ounce boneless chicken breasts, trimmed of fat

1. In a large bowl, combine the marmalade, onion, Pickapeppa sauce, butter, and cheese and stir together well. Add the chicken breasts, cover, and refrigerate for at least 2 hours—overnight if possible.

2. Preheat the oven to 400°F or heat an outdoor grill. Remove the chicken from the refrigerator and place each piece in a flat bowl of aluminum foil. Cover with the marmalade sauce and leave the top of the bowl open.

3. Place the chicken in the oven or on the grill and cook for 15 to 20 minutes or until fully cooked. If cooking in the oven, place the chicken under the broiler for the last 5 minutes to brown the top. Serve immediately.

Serves 4

Chicken

STOLEN JAMAICAN CHICKEN *(Jamaica)*

Our chef was inspired by a trip to Jamaica when he created this recipe. It combines fresh herbs, citrus, and vermouth with Dijon mustard for juicy and flavorful results.

Jamaica

The third largest of the Caribbean islands, Jamaica is the best known and most visited by tourists. It is an ideal vacation spot. With more than half of the island 1,000 feet above sea level, it offers the drama of lush tropical mountains, some as high as 7,400 feet, cascading to the crystalline waters below, and bejeweled with waterfalls, caves, and colorful reefs. The cuisine of Jamaica mirrors its culture, values, history, and mode of expression. Roadside food vendors offer a variety of traditional foods, especially fiery beef patties and jerk dishes. Island specialties include rice and peas and spicy hot curries. The language is officially English, but a heavy patois of Spanish, Creole, English, and African is spoken among the locals.

MARINADE:

- ¼ cup lime juice
- ¼ cup lemon juice
- ¼ cup white cooking wine
- 2 tablespoons Dijon mustard
- ¼ teaspoon ground cumin
- ¼ teaspoon dried thyme
- ¼ teaspoon dried basil
- ¼ teaspoon dried oregano
- 1 teaspoon Old Bay Seasoning
- ¼ teaspoon freshly ground black pepper
- ¼ cup Worcestershire sauce
- ¼ cup sweet vermouth
- ¼ teaspoon dried parsley

- 4 6- to 8-ounce chicken breasts, trimmed of fat
- 2 tablespoons Dijon mustard
- 1½ tablespoons butter

1. In a large bowl, combine all the ingredients for the marinade. Mix well, making sure that the mustard blends smoothly with the liquids and spices. Add the chicken breasts, cover, and refrigerate for at least 1 hour.

2. Preheat the oven to 350°F. Remove the chicken breasts from the marinade and set the marinade aside. Rub each breast with Dijon mustard and butter and place in a 9 × 13-inch baking dish. Pour the marinade on top and bake for 45 minutes, basting occasionally.

3. Transfer the chicken to a serving platter and pour the drippings into a gravy boat and serve as a sauce. Accompany with lots of French bread.

Serves 4

101

GRILLED CHICKEN WITH HAVANA SAUCE *(Cuba)*

T he key to this sensational dish is the sauce. Here it is served over grilled chicken, but it can be used on just about anything. Prepare the sauce a day ahead and let it stand overnight in the refrigerator to blend the flavors. You might like to prepare extra and freeze what you don't use right away.

SAUCE:

- 1 28-ounce can plum tomatoes, drained and roughly chopped
- ⅓ cup olive oil
- ¼ cup white wine
- 1 tablespoon white vinegar
- 3 green onions, finely chopped
- 4 cloves garlic, minced
- ½ teaspoon salt
- ½ teaspoon freshly ground black pepper
- 2 teaspoons minced fresh coriander

- 8 6- to 8-ounce chicken breasts, skin removed

  Juice of 2 limes

  Salt to taste

  Freshly ground black pepper to taste

1. In a large bowl, combine all the ingredients for the sauce. Mix well, cover, and refrigerate overnight.

2. Heat an outdoor grill and let the sauce come to room temperature. Sprinkle the chicken breasts with the lime juice and with salt and pepper as you like. Place on the grill and cook for about 6 minutes per side or until browned. Brush the sauce on the breasts throughout the grilling and top each with more sauce when serving.

Serves 8

Chicken

LEMON CHICKEN

A distinctive Chinese flavor characterizes this dish, which combines chicken with a tangy citrus sauce. Serve it the traditional Chinese way—hot over a bed of crisp lettuce.

1 pound boneless chicken, cut into ½-inch cubes
½ teaspoon salt
1 tablespoon dark rum
1 tablespoon soy sauce
½ teaspoon sugar
2 eggs, beaten
¼ cup cornstarch
½ teaspoon baking powder
Oil for deep frying
Lettuce leaves, for garnish
Lemon slices, for garnish

LEMON SAUCE:
1 tablespoon oil
1 teaspoon salt
3 teaspoons sugar
1 tablespoon cornstarch
2 tablespoons lemon juice
1 cup chicken stock

1. Rub the chicken pieces with the salt and briefly set aside. In a shallow bowl, combine the rum, soy sauce, and sugar. Add the chicken pieces and stir well to coat. Cover the bowl and refrigerate for at least 30 minutes.

2. In a separate bowl, combine the eggs, cornstarch, and baking powder. Beat the mixture with a whisk until smooth and briefly set aside. Preheat the oil in a deep fryer to 375°F.

3. To make the lemon sauce, heat the oil in a heavy saucepan and slowly stir in the salt, sugar, cornstarch, lemon juice, and chicken stock. Stir constantly until the sauce becomes thicker and clear. Keep warm.

4. Remove the chicken from the marinade and discard the liquid. Dip each piece in the batter and shake off any excess. Deep-fry the pieces, about 6 at a time, for 4 to 5 minutes. Drain on paper towels and keep warm. Line a serving platter with lettuce leaves, arrange the chicken on top, and surround with slices of lemon. Pour the hot lemon sauce over the chicken and serve immediately.

Serves 4 as an appetizer
Serves 2 as an entree

Lemon Tree
Traditional

Lemon tree, very
pretty
And the lemon flower is
sweet,
But the fruit of the
poor lemon
Is impossible to eat.
When I was a young
lad of ten,
Father said to me,
Come here and take a
lesson from
The lovely lemon tree.
Don't put your trust in
love, my boy,
Father said to me.
I fear you will find that
love is like
A lovely lemon tree.

CURRIED CHICKEN IN COCONUT *(Jamaica)*

This is a fine example of Jamaican cuisine. It is a popular dish full of rich curry and coconut flavors. For especially authentic results, try making it with Jamaican curry powder (page 11).

2	tablespoons olive oil
1½	pounds boneless chicken breasts, trimmed of fat and cubed
1	cup chicken stock
1	cup dry white wine
¼	cup curry powder
1	tablespoon salt
1	tablespoon freshly ground black pepper
3	green peppers, seeded and cut into ¼-inch strips
3	carrots, thinly sliced
1	cup coconut cream (page 10)
1	cup unsweetened shredded coconut
2	tablespoons cornstarch stirred into ¼ cup water

1. In a large heavy skillet, heat the olive oil, add the cubed chicken, and brown on all sides for about 5 minutes. Add the chicken stock, wine, curry powder, salt, and pepper and stir well. Let this simmer over moderate heat, stirring occasionally, for about 5 minutes.

2. Stir in the green peppers, carrots, coconut cream, and ½ cup of the shredded coconut. Simmer again for about 10 minutes, stirring occasionally, or until the vegetables are tender. Add enough of the cornstarch to thicken the sauce. Serve on individual plates with Calabaza Pumpkin Rice (page 152) and garnish with the remaining shredded coconut.

Serves 4

Chicken

TROPICAL FLAUTAS DE POLLO

This dish was tested at Sugar Reef as a special by Pablo and was an instant success. It combines coconut, bananas, strawberries, and rum in a spectacular sauce that is ladled over fried chicken cutlets.

3 eggs

1 tablespoon salt

1 tablespoon freshly ground black pepper

1 cup flour

4 cups sweetened shredded coconut

8 3-ounce boneless breasts of chicken

8 ripe bananas, peeled

Oil for deep frying

1 cup frozen strawberries

¼ cup lime juice

2 tablespoons dark rum

1. In a shallow bowl, beat the eggs with the salt and pepper. Spread the flour and coconut on separate plates. Lightly coat each chicken breast with the flour, then dip into the egg. Wrap the breast around a banana and roll the chicken and banana in the coconut. Cover completely, then lightly shake off any excess coconut. Refrigerate the chicken, uncovered, for 30 minutes.

2. Preheat the oil in a deep fryer to 350°F. In a blender or food processor, puree the strawberries, lime juice, and rum. Briefly set aside.

3. Deep-fry the chicken breasts, two at a time, until the coconut is golden brown, about 3 to 5 minutes. Drain on paper towels. Top with the strawberry sauce and serve immediately.

Serves 8

CALYPSO CHICKEN

Like calypso music, this recipe is a mélange of exotic ingredients that work together in perfect harmony. It combines cognac with passion fruit (in the Alizé), ginger with garlic, raisins with lime, and pineapple with chicken. The results will have your guests calypsoing for more.

4 pounds boneless chicken breasts, skin removed, cut in half

¼ cup lime juice

Grated rind of 1 lime

¼ cup lemon juice

1½ cups Alizé liqueur

1 cup dark raisins

½ cup (1 stick) butter

2 cups finely chopped green onions

2 cloves garlic, minced

1¾ cups pineapple chunks (1 small to medium pineapple or 1 14-ounce can)

2 teaspoons Worcestershire sauce

½ teaspoon ground ginger

¼ teaspoon ground cinnamon

1 teaspoon salt

Chopped pimientos, for garnish

1. Marinate the chicken breasts in the lime juice, lime rind, lemon juice, and 1 cup of the Alizé for at least 30 minutes. At the same time, soak the raisins in the remaining ½ cup Alizé.

2. Preheat the oven to 350°F. Remove the chicken from the marinade and reserve the liquid. Melt the butter in a heavy 10-inch skillet over moderate heat and sauté the green onions and garlic until limp. Add the chicken breasts and sauté until they begin to turn white.

3. Place the chicken breasts in an ungreased 4-quart casserole or baking dish with the sautéed onions and garlic. Add the raisins and their liquid and all the remaining ingredients to the reserved marinade, stir to combine, and pour over the chicken. Bake, uncovered, for 45 minutes. Garnish with chopped pimientos and serve with saffron rice.

Serves 8

Chicken

CHICKEN CROQUETTES *(Dominican Republic)*

G reat as an entree or an appetizer, these golden morsels are perfect topped by our snappy Red Pepper Remoulade. You can prepare the croquettes ahead of time and deep-fry them just before serving.

3 tablespoons olive oil

2 tablespoons chopped white onion

2 tablespoons chopped red pepper

2 tablespoons chopped fresh parsley

1 teaspoon salt

1 teaspoon freshly ground black pepper

2 tablespoons minced smoked ham

1¼ cups flour

1 cup milk

2 cups ground chicken (about 1 pound)

¼ teaspoon ground nutmeg

2 eggs, beaten

1½ cups seasoned bread crumbs

Oil for frying

Lettuce leaves, for garnish

Tomato slices, for garnish

Lime wedges, for garnish

1. In a large saucepan, heat the olive oil and add the onion, red pepper, parsley, salt, black pepper, and ham. Sauté the ingredients over moderate heat for about 3 minutes, then slowly add ¼ cup of the flour, stirring to mix in and prevent the flour from browning. Add the milk and stir until the mixture thickens. Add the chicken and nutmeg and let the mixture simmer, stirring occasionally, for 2 minutes. Transfer the chicken to a large bowl and allow it to cool to room temperature, about 20 minutes.

2. When the chicken has cooled, scoop up enough of the mixture to roll into a golf-ball-size croquette. Roll each piece in the remaining 1 cup flour and dip into the beaten egg. Finish by rolling the croquettes in the bread crumbs. Preheat the oil in a deep fryer to 350°F.

3. Place 4 to 6 croquettes at a time in the deep fryer and cook until they are golden brown, about 6 minutes. Drain on paper towels and place immediately on a platter lined with lettuce leaves. Garnish with tomato slices and lime wedges. Top the croquettes with Red Pepper Remoulade (page 193) or serve the sauce in a small bowl for dipping.

4 servings (20 croquettes)

Beef & Pork

STEAK FRITE

T he French have been preparing steak this way for centuries, and the people of the French West Indies have adopted the method as their own, but with a few island twists.

4   6- to 8-ounce sirloin steaks, trimmed of fat

4   cloves garlic, minced

1   tablespoon salt

1   tablespoon freshly ground black pepper

2   limes

Butter

1. On a sturdy countertop pound the steaks with a heavy mallet. Pound them as thin as possible without breaking the meat.

2. Rub each steak with the garlic, salt, and black pepper. Squeeze the juice from the limes over the steaks. Place the steaks on a platter, cover, and refrigerate for at least 40 minutes.

3. Heat a heavy iron skillet until hot and melt enough butter to fry the steaks without sticking. Cook each steak for 5 to 6 minutes on each side or until brown. Serve immediately.

Serves 4

Beef & Pork

POPPA RUE'S MANGO STEAK

This simple recipe is a Sugar Reef creation, named for our favorite taste tester, Russell. The mango can be replaced with any fruit in season, and the remaining ingredients are available year round.

¼ cup (½ stick) unsalted butter

1 green mango, peeled, pitted, and cubed

1 Spanish onion, finely chopped

3 green onions, finely chopped

1 teaspoon chopped Scotch bonnet pepper

1 green pepper, seeded and finely chopped

2 cloves garlic, minced

1 large tomato, finely chopped

½ cup Worcestershire sauce

1 tablespoon prepared yellow mustard

1 8-ounce jar mango chutney, chopped

Juice of 1 lime

6 tablespoons mango nectar

1 teaspoon salt

1 teaspoon freshly ground black pepper

4 8- to 10-ounce sirloin strip steaks, trimmed of fat

1. Preheat an outdoor grill. In a large heavy skillet, melt the butter and sauté the mango, onion, green onions, Scotch bonnet pepper, green pepper, garlic, and tomato until the vegetables are limp. Add the Worcestershire sauce, mustard, chutney, lime juice, and mango nectar and stir well to combine. Bring the sauce to a boil, lower the heat, and simmer for 15 to 20 minutes.

2. Remove the sauce from the stove and place it in a serving bowl. Salt and pepper the steaks and grill for 5 minutes on one side. Turn and top the cooked side with a large spoonful of the mango sauce. Grill for another 5 minutes or until the steaks are fully cooked. Serve hot with the remaining sauce.

Serves 4

BIFTECK AIOLI

A steak prepared with the French Caribbean touch. For a truly impressive meal, serve it with Broiled Artichoke Hearts and Tomatoes (page 142).

6   8-ounce boneless strip steaks
1   tablespoon olive oil
2   tablespoons dark rum
1   teaspoon salt
1   teaspoon freshly ground black pepper
2   tablespoons chopped white onion
3   tablespoons minced garlic
1   tablespoon finely chopped fresh parsley
2   tablespoons finely chopped red pepper
2   teaspoons lime juice
¼   cup white vinegar
2   egg yolks
1   cup olive oil
1   red onion, sliced
2   tablespoons butter
    Tomato slices, for garnish

1. Slightly pound each steak with a mallet to tenderize. Mix the olive oil, rum, salt, and black pepper, rub on the steaks, and marinate at room temperature for 30 minutes.

2. In a large bowl, combine the onion, garlic, parsley, red pepper, lime juice, and vinegar. Whisk in the egg yolks until fully combined, then add in the olive oil in a slow and steady stream. Continue to whisk until the mixture is the consistency of mayonnaise. For a thicker sauce, add another egg yolk.

3. In a skillet over moderate heat, sauté the onion in the butter until limp. Remove from the skillet and briefly set aside. The steaks can be pan-fried or grilled on an outdoor grill. Top each cooked steak with the garlic sauce and add the onions. Garnish with tomato slices.

Serves 6

Beef & Pork

BEEF IN GARLIC SAUCE

Like so many Spanish dishes made with meat, this recipe is dominated by garlic and studded with olives and capers. We serve it with sweet plantains for contrasting tastes.

St. John

The Virgin Islands were named for St. Ursula and the 11,000 virgins killed by Huns in the Middle Ages. There are more than 50 islands, islets, and cays in the U.S. Virgin Islands. Among them, St. John is said to be the most tranquil and least disturbed. To a large extent Laurance Rockefeller can be thanked for this, for in 1956 he purchased about 5,000 acres of land on the island and turned it over to the National Park Service, hoping to preserve the distinct beauty of St. John. Although residents of the Virgin Islands have a tradition of not claiming one island to be superior to any other—saying each has something very different to offer—St. John is known as Love City, surrounded by the spirit of 11,000 beautiful virgins.

1   4-pound eye of round roast (about 3½ pounds trimmed)
1   tablespoon salt
1   tablespoon freshly ground black pepper
¼   cup olive oil
1   small white onion, thinly sliced
1   bulb (whole head) garlic, minced
½   cup chopped green olives with pimientos
½   cup chopped capers
   Juice of 3 limes
¼   cup sugar
6   cups water
3   potatoes, peeled and cut into ¼-inch slices

1. Rub the roast with the salt and pepper. In a large Dutch oven, heat the olive oil and sauté the onion and garlic until they become limp. Add the roast and brown on all sides. Add the olives, capers, lime juice, sugar, and water. Stir the ingredients and bring to a rapid boil over high heat. Lower the heat and simmer, covered, for 2 hours, turning the meat every 45 minutes.

2. Turn the heat up and add the potatoes. Bring to a rapid boil once again and stir well. Lower the heat, cover, and simmer for another hour, turning the meat after half an hour.

3. Uncover and continue to simmer until the sauce thickens and the meat is fork tender, about 10 minutes. Slice the meat and serve it with the sauce over white rice.

Serves 6

ROPA VIEJA

Old clothes is the English translation of this recipe's name. Actually it's shredded pot roast in a tomato sauce full of onions, peppers, olives, and capers. Try serving it with wedges of fresh avocado.

2 tablespoons olive oil

1 red onion, finely chopped

1 white onion, finely chopped

1 green pepper, seeded and finely chopped

4 sprigs fresh coriander, roughly chopped

4 cloves garlic, minced

1 5-pound boneless chuck roast

1 teaspoon salt

1 teaspoon freshly ground black pepper

¾ cup water

2 cups tomato sauce

2 tablespoons chopped green olives

1 tablespoon chopped capers

1. Heat the olive oil in a large Dutch oven and sauté the onions, green pepper, coriander, and garlic until tender but not brown.

2. Rub the beef with the salt and pepper and add to the Dutch oven. Brown on all sides for 15 to 20 minutes. Add the water, tomato sauce, olives, and capers and stir well. Bring the mixture to a simmer and lower the heat. Cook over low heat for 1 to 1½ hours. The meat should pull apart easily.

3. Before serving, shred the pot roast with a fork. Serve the meat and sauce over white rice.

Serves 6

Beef & Pork

BEEF SATAY *(Curaçao)*

A sauce made of peanut butter, fresh ginger, lime juice, and red pepper reflects the variety of cultural influences on Caribbean cooking. The Africans introduced the peanut, and the Asians introduced ginger.

Curaçao

Situated just 35 miles off the coast of Venezuela, Curaçao was discovered by Amerigo Vespucci in 1499. Throughout the island's history many different groups of people have come together. Today the population is descended from early African slaves, Dutch merchants and planters, and Spanish and Portuguese Jews. Linguists marvel at the conglomerate language, called Papiamento, which is a blending of several languages including African, Portuguese, Dutch, French, and Spanish, with a few important words from English thrown in, such as payday, watch out, and okay. The island is famous for its Amstel beer, brewed from desalinated water, and Curaçao, a liqueur made from the skins of local oranges.

MARINADE:

1	cup lime juice
4	cloves garlic, minced
½	cup soy sauce
2	tablespoons peanut oil
1½	teaspoons salt
1½	teaspoons freshly ground black pepper
1	tablespoon grated fresh ginger

SAUCE:

¾	cup unsweetened peanut butter
½	cup lemon juice
¼	cup soy sauce
1	tablespoon red pepper flakes
2	cloves garlic, minced
1	tablespoon sugar
1	tablespoon ground ginger
½	cup warm water

2	pounds boneless lean beef, cubed
1	large white onion, cut into large chunks
2	red peppers, seeded and cut into squares
2	green peppers, seeded and cut into squares

1. In a large bowl, combine the ingredients for the marinade and add the beef. Cover the bowl and refrigerate for at least 1 hour.

2. In a food processor or blender, place the ingredients for the sauce and process until smooth and thoroughly combined. If the sauce is too thick, add up to ½ cup warm water. Store the sauce in the refrigerator until ready to use.

3. Preheat an outdoor grill. Drain the beef, setting aside ¼ cup of the marinade. Alternate the beef cubes on skewers with pieces of onion, red pepper, and green pepper. Place the skewers on a long platter and pour the marinade on top. When the grill is hot, brown the beef for 15 to 20 minutes, turning occasionally, until it is fully cooked. Liberally coat with the peanut sauce and serve with hot white rice.

Serves 4

SPANISH STUFFED PEPPERS

R aisins, capers, olives, and garlic always make for an interesting stuffing. In this recipe we add ground beef and tomato sauce and stuff it in sweet green peppers. They can be made in advance and stored in the refrigerator.

1 pound lean ground beef

1 white onion, finely chopped

3 cloves garlic, minced

½ cup finely chopped pimiento-stuffed green olives

½ cup finely chopped capers

½ cup dark raisins

1 teaspoon chopped Scotch bonnet pepper

1 8-ounce can tomato sauce

Salt to taste

6 green peppers, tops removed and seeded

1. In a large skillet, brown the ground beef. Add the onion, garlic, olives, and capers. Sauté until the vegetables are tender and the beef is fully cooked. Drain off any excess fat. Add the raisins, Scotch bonnet pepper, and tomato sauce and stir well to combine. Season to taste with salt and simmer until all the liquid evaporates.

2. Preheat the oven to 350°F. Stuff each green pepper with the ground beef mixture and arrange them in a small baking pan. Pour ½ cup hot water into the pan and bake in a slow oven until the peppers are tender and the stuffing is bubbly, about 1 hour.

Serves 6

Beef & Pork

MEAT PATTIES *(Jamaica)*

The Spanish call their delectable meat pies *pasteles*. In the islands the patties were transformed to utilize native ingredients, such as potatoes, plaintains, and bananas. The frugal Indian and African population saved scraps of meat left over from meals, ground them up with seasonings, and enclosed them in pastry.

PASTRY:
- 2 **cups flour**
- ¼ **teaspoon salt**
- ¼ **cup solid shortening**
- ¼ **cup (½ stick) margarine**
- ⅓ **cup cold water**

MEAT FILLING:
- 2 **tablespoons margarine**
- 1 **small white onion, finely chopped**
- ¼ **teaspoon chopped Scotch bonnet pepper**
- ½ **pound lean ground beef**
- ½ **teaspoon salt**
- ½ **teaspoon freshly ground black pepper**
- ½ **teaspoon curry powder**
- ½ **teaspoon dried thyme**
- ¼ **cup bread crumbs**
- ¼ **cup beef or chicken stock**

- 1 **egg, beaten**
- ¼ **cup water**

1. Sift the flour and salt into a large bowl. Cut in the shortening and margarine until crumbly. Add the cold water to make a stiff dough. Lightly flour a wooden cutting board and roll out the dough until about ⅛ inch thick. Cut out 8-inch circles. Cover with wax paper or a damp cloth towel until ready to use.

2. In a heavy skillet, melt the margarine and sauté the onion and Scotch bonnet pepper until they become limp. Add the ground beef, salt, pepper, curry powder, and thyme and mix well. Brown the meat for about 10 minutes, stirring occasionally.

3. Add the bread crumbs and the stock and combine all the ingredients well. Cover the skillet and simmer for about 10 to 15 minutes, stirring occasionally. When all the liquids have been absorbed, the filling is ready. It should be moist but not watery. Remove the skillet from the stove and preheat the oven to 400°F.

4. Uncover the dough circles and place 2 to 3 tablespoons of filling on each half. Moisten the edges of the dough with water and fold the remaining half over the meat filling. Pinch the edges closed with a fork. Lightly brush the pastry with a mixture of the egg and water. Bake on a lightly greased baking sheet for 30 to 40 minutes or until the pastry is golden brown.

Yield: 10 patties

Hambone
Afro-Carib song

Ham-bone, ham-bone,
* where you been?*
Round the world and
* back again.*
Hambone, hambone,
* where's your wife?*
In the kitchen cooking
* rice.*

PICADILLO *(Cuba)*

I f anything could be called the national dish of Cuba, this would be it. Laced with fragrant spices, Picadillo is delicious not only as a main course but also as a stuffing for *roti* bread.

1 large white onion, chopped

2 cloves garlic, minced

2 tablespoons olive oil

2 pounds lean ground beef

1 large can (12 ounces) tomato paste

1 cup water

10 to 15 pimiento-stuffed green olives, sliced

¾ cup dark raisins

1 tablespoon salt

1 teaspoon freshly ground black pepper

1 teaspoon dried oregano

1 teaspoon dried tarragon

In a large skillet over moderate heat, sauté the onion and garlic in the oil until they are limp; remove and set aside. Add the ground beef to the oil remaining in the skillet and cook, stirring, until completely browned, about 5 minutes. Return the onion and garlic to the pan and stir in the tomato paste, water, olives, raisins, salt, pepper, oregano, and tarragon. Lower the heat and simmer, covered, for about 3 hours (the longer, the better). Serve with white rice and Black Beans (page 155).

Serves 4

Beef & Pork

KESHI YENA *(Curaçao)*

This beef and vegetable pie, which originated in Curaçao, perfectly illustrates the Dutch influence upon Caribbean cuisine. Its name is derived from the Papiamento language, a blending of Spanish, Portuguese, Dutch, English, and African that is the *patois* of the Netherland Antilles.

¼ cup (½ stick) butter

1 white onion, finely chopped

2 cloves garlic, minced

1 green pepper, seeded and finely chopped

2 dill pickles, finely chopped

1 large tomato, cubed

3 tablespoons chopped green olives

1 tablespoon chopped capers

½ cup dark raisins

1 pound lean ground beef, cooked and drained

½ cup Pickapeppa sauce

1 teaspoon yellow mustard

1 teaspoon dried thyme

1 teaspoon freshly ground black pepper

¾ pound Edam cheese, thinly sliced

1. In a heavy skillet, melt the butter and sauté the onion, garlic, and green pepper until limp. Transfer to a large bowl.

2. Add the pickles, tomato, olives, capers, raisins, and cooked ground beef and mix well. Stir in the Pickapeppa sauce, mustard, thyme, and pepper. Preheat the oven to 350°F.

3. Line the bottom and sides of a greased deep 10-inch pie pan with three-fourths of the cheese. Spread the meat and vegetable mixture evenly over the cheese and cover with the remaining cheese. Bake for 30 minutes.

4. Before serving, let the pie cool for 15 to 20 minutes. This allows the cheese to solidify a bit before slicing.

Serves 6

Dutch Architecture

The architecture in The Netherland Antilles is Dutch, and the buildings are renowned for the vibrant colors on their facades, a custom begun by an early colonial governor. The extreme glare that reflected off the white buildings due to the strong Caribbean sun gave him severe headaches, and he ordered that they all be painted bright pastel shades.

GRILLED PORK CHOPS WITH MANGO CHUTNEY

Chutney is a perfect match with meats—it complements without masking the flavors. This simple recipe is a combination of Caribbean ideas put together by our chef.

4 6-ounce loin pork chops
   Juice of 4 limes

4 cloves garlic, minced

1 cup mango chutney, chopped

1. Place the pork chops in a shallow dish and add the lime juice and garlic. Cover and marinate in the refrigerator for at least 1 hour.

2. Preheat an outdoor grill. Remove the chops from the marinade and grill for 8 to 10 minutes on each side, basting liberally with the chutney. Be sure to save some chutney for serving.

3. Remove the chops and serve with a spoonful of chutney on the side.

Serves 4

Beef & Pork

PORK CHOPS ETOUFFÉE

Pork is a favorite meat in the French West Indies, where it is prepared in a creative and very different way than on other islands. This dish is excellent with Island Yams (page 150) and fresh green beans.

Juice of 2 limes
4 cloves garlic, minced
1 teaspoon salt
1 teaspoon freshly ground black pepper
1 Scotch bonnet pepper, seeded and finely chopped
4 6- to 8-ounce loin pork chops, trimmed of fat
½ cup sugar
¼ cup annatto oil or vegetable oil
2 sprigs fresh parsley, finely chopped
3 green onions, finely chopped (including green)
1 teaspoon dried thyme
¼ cup hot water

1. In a shallow bowl, combine the lime juice, garlic, salt, black pepper, and Scotch bonnet pepper. Add the pork chops, turn to coat well, and refrigerate, covered, for at least 40 minutes.

2. Heat a heavy iron skillet until very hot and add the sugar. Let it melt and turn brown, then pour the annatto oil on top. When this becomes bubbly, add the pork chops and brown. Cook on each side for about 5 minutes.

3. When the pork chops have browned on both sides, add the parsley, green onions, and thyme. Stir well and slowly add the hot water. Be careful—the water will splatter and sizzle for a few seconds. Let the sauce simmer over low heat until thick, about 15 minutes, then serve the pork chops with the sauce spooned over them.

Serves 4

"JERK" PORK CHOPS

Proper marination is the most important step in preparing this recipe. If you like, you can give the sauce more punch by doubling the dried ingredients, but be sure to have lots of water standing by to cool the fires.

- 1 tablespoon ground allspice
- 1 tablespoon dried thyme
- 1½ teaspoons cayenne pepper
- 1½ teaspoons freshly ground black pepper
- 1½ teaspoons ground sage
- ¾ teaspoon ground nutmeg
- ¾ teaspoon ground cinnamon
- 2 tablespoons salt
- 2 tablespoons garlic powder
- 1 tablespoon sugar
- ¼ cup olive oil
- ¼ cup soy sauce
- ¾ cup white vinegar
- ¼ cup orange juice
- Juice of 1 lime
- 1 Scotch bonnet pepper, seeded and finely chopped
- 1 cup chopped white onion
- 3 green onions, finely chopped
- 4 6- to 8-ounce pork chops

1. In a large bowl, combine the allspice, thyme, cayenne pepper, black pepper, sage, nutmeg, cinnamon, salt, garlic powder, and sugar. With a wire whisk, mix in the olive oil, soy sauce, vinegar, orange juice, and lime juice. Add the Scotch bonnet pepper, white onion, and green onions. Stir well and add the pork chops. Cover and marinate for at least 1 hour, longer if possible.

2. Preheat an outdoor grill. Remove the pork chops from the marinade and grill for 8 to 10 minutes on each side or until fully cooked. While grilling, liberally baste with the marinade. Heat the extra sauce until bubbly and serve on the side for dipping.

Serves 4

Beef & Pork

CHULETAS SALSA NEGRA

ur chef Pablo created this rich pork entree. He marinates the chops, then smothers them in a fragrant sauce made with beer, tomato sauce, and minced vegetables.

4   6- to 8-ounce pork chops
1   teaspoon salt
1   teaspoon freshly ground black pepper
2   tablespoons olive oil
1   green pepper, seeded
1   small white onion
4   green onions
1   stalk celery
1   clove garlic
¼   cup sugar
1   tablespoon water
2   teaspoons flour
1   12-ounce bottle dark beer
6   tablespoons Worcestershire sauce
½   cup tomato sauce

1. Rub the pork chops with the salt and pepper. Heat the olive oil in a heavy large skillet. When hot, fry the pork chops until fully cooked, about 6 to 8 minutes on each side. Remove the chops and keep them warm on a platter in the oven. Set the skillet aside.

2. In a food processor or by hand, chop the green pepper, white onion, green onions, celery, and garlic very fine. Set aside.

3. Return the skillet to the stove over medium heat. When hot, add the sugar and stir until it starts to melt. Add the water and keep stirring. When the water has completely combined with the sugar, add the flour. Stirring constantly, let this mixture get very brown, about 2 to 3 minutes. Add the beer, Worcestershire sauce, tomato sauce, and chopped vegetables. Cook over low heat for 10 minutes, stirring. Add the pork chops to the pan and completely cover in the sauce. Simmer for about 5 minutes and serve.

Serves 4

CHULETAS EMPAÑADAS *(Dominican Republic)*

L atin-style fried pork chops are especially good topped with Salsa Naranja, but you can serve these crispy, juicy morsels with any favorite sauce.

3 eggs

1 teaspoon salt

1 teaspoon freshly ground black pepper

1 cup flour

1 cup seasoned bread crumbs

6 3-ounce boneless pork chops

2 tablespoons oil

1. In a shallow bowl, beat the eggs with the salt and pepper. Spread the flour and bread crumbs on separate plates. Lightly coat each pork chop with the flour, then dip into the egg and roll in the bread crumbs to cover completely. Briefly set aside.

2. In a heavy skillet, heat the oil over medium-high heat. Add the chops and fry until golden brown, about 3 minutes on each side. Drain on paper towels. Top with Salsa Naranja (page 190) and serve immediately.

Serves 6

Beef & Pork

CREOLE PORK CHOPS *(Dominican Republic)*

 Fresh herbs make these pork chops a hit. Our chef Pablo has combined fresh basil and rosemary with a delicate blend of ingredients.

¼ cup olive oil

2 cloves garlic, minced

1 red onion, finely chopped

2 beefsteak tomatoes, sliced

4 sprigs fresh basil, finely chopped

1 sprig fresh rosemary, finely chopped

2 tablespoons tomato paste

¼ cup water

¼ cup dry white wine

1 tablespoon Dijon mustard

6 2- to 3-ounce boneless pork chops

   Salt to taste

   Freshly ground black pepper to taste

   Chopped rosemary and basil, for garnish

1. In a large heavy skillet, heat the olive oil over moderate heat and add the garlic, onion, and tomatoes. Cook and stir the ingredients for about 3 minutes or until the tomatoes start to fall apart. Add the basil, rosemary, and tomato paste and stir well to combine the ingredients. Add the water and bring the sauce to a simmer. Cook until it begins to thicken, about 2 minutes, then stir in the wine and mustard.

2. When the sauce is smooth, add the pork chops and cover with the sauce. Simmer the chops over medium to low heat for 8 to 10 minutes. The sauce will thicken and stick to the chops. If the sauce begins to dry out, add more wine. Season with salt and pepper and serve on a bed of white rice. Spoon any remaining sauce on top and garnish with the fresh herbs.

Serves 6

NOT QUITE ANNA'S PERNIL *(Jamaica)*

We sampled this mouth-watering dish at a restaurant in Jamaica and pleaded with the chef for the recipe, but to no avail. We liked it so much that we created our own version, which is very good. However, it's not quite Anna's pernil.

1   **4- to 5-pound loin pork roast**

2   **tablespoons olive oil**

4   **cloves garlic, sliced**

1   **teaspoon salt**

1   **teaspoon freshly ground black pepper**

1   **small white onion, finely chopped**

1   **tablespoon dried oregano**

1   **tablespoon sweet paprika**

1   **tablespoon ground annatto seed (optional)**

4   **sprigs fresh coriander, finely chopped**

¼   **cup lemon juice**

¼   **cup white vinegar**

½   **cup chicken stock**

2   **teaspoons cornstarch stirred into 2 tablespoons water**

1. Rub the pork roast with the olive oil. With a knife, make little slits in the meat and insert the garlic slices. Sprinkle salt and pepper on the outside and briefly set aside.

2. In a large bowl, combine the onion, oregano, paprika, annatto seed, and coriander. Add the lemon juice and vinegar and stir well. Place the roast in this mixture, turn to coat well, and refrigerate, covered, overnight.

3. Preheat the oven to 350°F. Place the pork in a roasting pan and roast for 1 hour, basting occasionally. Remove from the oven and drain the drippings into a small bowl. Stir the chicken stock into the drippings, pour over the pork, and return to the oven. Roast for another 30 minutes, basting occasionally, or until the meat is fully cooked. Before serving, drain the drippings into a saucepan and thicken with the cornstarch to make a gravy.

Serves 4 to 6

Beef & Pork

PORK ROAST WITH HOLIDAY STUFFING

Christmas in the Caribbean is celebrated with as much joy and excitement as anywhere in the world. Families gather to dance and sing, and large meals are prepared with extra care. This is a fine example of traditional holiday fare in the tropics.

1 teaspoon salt

1 teaspoon freshly ground black pepper

1 3- to 4-pound pork roast

4 cloves garlic, sliced

½ cup brown sugar

¼ cup dark rum

3 tablespoons lime juice

1 bay leaf, crushed

1 teaspoon ground ginger

½ teaspoon ground cloves

¾ cup chicken stock

2 teaspoons cornstarch stirred into 2 tablespoons water

Lime slices, for garnish

Coriander or parsley leaves, for garnish

STUFFING:

3 cups bread crumbs

Milk, about ¾ cup

2 cloves garlic, minced

1 white onion, chopped

½ cup dark raisins

¼ cup chopped green olives

1 tablespoon chopped capers

1 teaspoon chopped Scotch bonnet pepper

1 large tomato, cubed

1 teaspoon dried thyme

2 tablespoons butter

1. Preheat the oven to 350°F. Sprinkle the salt and pepper over the pork roast. With a knife, make small slits in the meat and insert the garlic slices. In a small bowl, combine the brown sugar, 2 tablespoons of the rum, 1 tablespoon of the lime juice, the bay leaf, ginger, and cloves to form a paste. Rub this over the pork and place it on a baking pan. Roast for 1 hour.

2. Meanwhile, make the stuffing. In a large bowl, moisten the bread crumbs with the milk. Mix in the remaining ingredients and set aside.

3. Remove the pork from the oven and drain the drippings into a small bowl. Add the chicken stock and stir well. Arrange the stuffing around the pork and pour one-fourth of the stock and drippings mixture over the pork and stuffing. Return to the oven and roast for another 30 minutes. Baste if necessary after 20 minutes.

4. In a small saucepan, heat the remaining 2 tablespoons of rum and ignite. Let the flame burn for about 30 seconds and blow it out. Slowly add the remaining 2 tablespoons of lime juice, then the remaining stock and drippings mixture. Add the cornstarch and stir until the gravy thickens. Set aside and keep warm.

5. Remove the pork from the oven and place it on a large serving platter. Spoon out the stuffing and arrange it around the roast. Garnish with fresh lime slices and coriander or parsley leaves. Serve with the gravy.

Serves 4 to 6

GARLIC PORK *(Guyana)*

This method of preparing pork is unusual but incredibly tasty. In the Caribbean the meat is often marinated for as long as three or four days.

- 4 **pounds boneless lean pork, cubed**
- 4 **cups water**
- 1 **tablespoon salt**
- 1 **tablespoon freshly ground black pepper**
- 2 **cups white vinegar**
- 1 **bulb (whole head) garlic, minced**
- 1 **bunch fresh thyme, finely chopped**
- 4 **whole cloves**

1. Place the pork in a large bowl and add the remaining ingredients. Stir to coat the meat well and refrigerate, covered, for at least 12 hours.

2. Pour off and strain 1 cup of the marinade and discard the rest. Place the pork in a large Dutch oven, add the marinade, and bring to a boil over high heat. Let boil until all the liquid evaporates and only the pork remains. Let the meat brown, stirring constantly, until fully cooked—about 15 minutes.

Serves 4 to 6

Beef & Pork

CURRIED GOAT

 Goat is very popular in the Caribbean, especially when prepared in a curry sauce. On any special occasion or holiday you are likely to find it gracing the tables of many homes. We can offer this dish only occasionally at Sugar Reef, however, because we are unable to get a steady supply of fresh goat meat.

Aruba

The third largest celebrant of Carnival, preceded by Brazil and Trinidad, this island is a melting pot of nationalities and cultures. Papiamento is widely spoken, although Dutch is the official language. Among the natural features are a bridge that was carved out of stone by the wind and sea and a bizarre rock formation called Ayo, which is balanced on top of a small rock. Aruba is filled with charming Dutch architecture, and its array of desert vegetation includes cacti, aloe, and sea grapes. Come and hear the steel bands play "Jump Up" and sample the pan bati, a beaten bread.

2 tablespoons white vinegar

Juice of 2 limes

1 teaspoon salt

1 teaspoon freshly ground black pepper

6 pounds lean boneless goat, cut into 3-inch cubes

2 tablespoons annatto oil or vegetable oil

3 cloves garlic, chopped

¼ cup curry powder

½ cup water

2 cups chicken stock

Bouquet garni (2 sprigs fresh thyme, 2 sprigs fresh parsley, 2 green onions, 1 bay leaf)

5 new potatoes, peeled and halved

3 carrots, sliced

Shredded coconut, for garnish

Raisins, for garnish

Chopped nuts, for garnish

1. In a large bowl, combine the vinegar, lime juice, salt, and pepper. Add the goat meat and marinate for at least 1 hour, covered and refrigerated.

2. In a large Dutch oven, heat the oil and sauté the garlic pieces until crisp. Drain the meat, setting aside ¼ cup of the marinade. Add the meat to the Dutch oven and brown for 15 to 20 minutes.

3. Meanwhile, in a small saucepan, combine the curry powder, marinade, and water. Let this simmer over low heat for 10 to 15 minutes, then remove the saucepan from the stove and set aside.

4. When the goat has browned, add the curry mixture to the Dutch oven and stir well to combine. Simmer, stirring occasionally, for about 15 minutes. Add the chicken stock and bouquet garni, raise the heat, and bring to a boil while stirring. Add the potatoes and carrots, bring back to a boil, lower the heat, and simmer until the goat is tender and the carrots and potatoes are cooked, about 1 hour. Remove the bouquet garni and serve over hot white rice. Top with shredded coconut, raisins, and chopped nuts.

Serves 8 to 10

Vegetables & Side Dishes

OKRA MÉLANGE

Okra is native to tropical Africa and was brought to the Western Hemisphere by slaves in the 1600s. Long, green, and pointed, this vegetable is also known as legumbre, gumbo, and lady fingers. Female slaves believed that okra possessed a special power—that eating excessive amounts of it would induce abortion. Today okra is simply enjoyed as a flavorful addition to stews, soups, and gumbos. In this preparation it is sautéed, then baked with a variety of spices and ingredients.

¼ cup olive oil

1 cup chopped white onion

½ cup minced garlic (about 1 bulb)

½ cup chopped celery

1 cup chopped green pepper

2 cups diced tomatoes

Freshly ground black pepper to taste

1 teaspoon salt

Juice of 1 lime

½ cup white wine

2 cups finely diced fresh okra

½ teaspoon finely chopped fresh parsley

Butter

½ cup bread crumbs

1. In a large heavy skillet, heat the olive oil over moderate heat. Add the onion, garlic, celery, and green pepper and sauté until the vegetables begin to brown. Add the tomatoes, black pepper, and salt and continue to stir until the tomatoes begin to shrink. Stir in the lime juice and wine and heat the mixture until it begins to boil. Add the okra and parsley, lower the heat, and cover. Allow the okra to simmer for about 30 minutes, stirring occasionally to prevent sticking.

2. Preheat the oven to 350°F and lightly grease a casserole dish. Transfer the mélange to the casserole, dot the top with butter, and sprinkle with bread crumbs. Bake until the top is crispy and brown, about 15 minutes. Serve immediately.

Serves 4 to 6

Vegetables & Side Dishes

CURRIED VEGETABLES IN COCONUT

 Curry mixed with coconut milk makes a wonderful foundation for any sauce. Add fresh vegetables and you have a sensational side dish or vegetarian entree.

Trinidad and Tobago

Three hills that are first visible when viewing Trinidad from the sea inspired Columbus when he named it. After its discovery it seems as though people from everywhere came to Trinidad—Africans, East Indians, British, Chinese, Portuguese, Syrians, Spanish, Lebanese, Corsicans, and French— giving the island the distinction of being one of the few truly multi-racial societies. This exotic combination of people makes the foods of this melting pot steam with flair. Trinidad is also the birthplace of the steel drum and calypso music, which is melodic poetry about life on this tropical island. In 1889 the island of Tobago, just to the north, joined with Trinidad to form one government.

1   **cup white wine**

1   **cup chicken stock**

¼ **cup curry powder**

1   **teaspoon salt**

1   **teaspoon freshly ground black pepper**

4   **green peppers, seeded and thinly sliced**

4   **carrots, thinly sliced**

1   **large red onion, halved and quartered**

½ **pound fresh green beans, ends removed**

1   **bunch green onions, finely chopped**

1   **cup coconut cream (page 10)**

1   **cup shredded coconut**

2   **teaspoons cornstarch stirred into 2 tablespoons water**

In a large heavy skillet, combine the wine, chicken stock, curry powder, salt, and pepper. Bring to a boil over medium heat and add the green peppers, carrots, onion, green beans, green onions, coconut cream, and ½ cup of the shredded coconut. Stir these ingredients to combine well and simmer over medium heat for 10 to 15 minutes or until the vegetables are tender. Add enough cornstarch to thicken the sauce and stir well. Serve with Calabaza Pumpkin Rice (page 152) and garnish with the remaining shredded coconut.

Serves 4

EGGPLANT CREOLE

A cornucopia of fresh vegetables and herbs, with the eggplant at the center, makes this a spectacular dish. In the Caribbean the eggplant is known by a variety of names—garden egg, melongene, berenjena, and aubergine.

½ cup diced smoked ham

¼ cup olive oil

½ cup chopped white onion

4 cloves garlic, minced

1 cup chopped green pepper

¼ cup chopped celery

3 cups peeled and cubed eggplant

4 cups diced tomatoes

1½ teaspoons chopped fresh basil

1½ teaspoons ground sage

2 teaspoons salt

2 teaspoons freshly ground black pepper

½ cup red wine

½ cup tomato sauce

Dash hot red pepper sauce

1. In a heavy skillet over moderate heat, brown the ham in the olive oil. Add the onion, garlic, green pepper, and celery and sauté until the onion is translucent, about 5 minutes.

2. Add the eggplant and tomatoes, stir well, and cook for about 10 minutes. Add the basil, sage, salt, black pepper, and wine. Stir until the mixture begins to boil, then add the tomato sauce and hot sauce. Simmer, uncovered, over low heat for 10 to 15 minutes or until most of the liquid has evaporated. Serve immediately over white rice.

Serves 4

Vegetables & Side Dishes

CREOLE STUFFED AUBERGINE

T he word *Creole* defines a culture born out of a melting pot of cultures. It combines influences of the African, Indian, and French populations and an array of styles and flavors in cooking. *Aubergine*, the French word for eggplant, is also the name given to the vegetable in England and therefore on the British islands.

St. Martin

The island of St. Martin is half French and half Dutch and features the best of both cultures. On the French side is the fabulous cuisine, and on the Dutch side is the beautiful architecture. Columbus discovered the island on Saint Martin's day and claimed it for Spain, but he left quickly because of hostile attacks by the native Indians. In the 1600s St. Martin was settled by the French and Dutch, who began growing tobacco and mining for salt. Restaurants on the island offer West Indian cuisine as well as many other types of food, and St. Martin is known as the restaurant capital of the Caribbean.

2   large eggplants, halved lengthwise

½   pound smoked sausage, chopped

1   white onion, finely chopped

4   green onions, finely chopped

2   cloves garlic, minced

1   Scotch bonnet pepper, seeded and finely chopped

½   green pepper, seeded and finely chopped

¼   cup (½ stick) butter

2   sprigs fresh parsley

½   pound large shrimp, peeled, deveined, and halved

½   teaspoon salt

½   teaspoon sweet paprika

½   teaspoon dried thyme

½   teaspoon freshly ground black pepper

1   cup seasoned bread crumbs

½   cup red wine

1. In a large stockpot or Dutch oven, boil the eggplants in salted water to cover for 20 to 30 minutes or until tender. Remove from the pot and drain. When the eggplants are cool, scoop out the pulp, leaving ¼-inch shells. Roughly chop the pulp and set aside.

2. In a heavy saucepan over medium heat, brown the sausage. When some fat has been rendered, add the white onion, green onions, garlic, and peppers. Sauté for 10 to 15 minutes or until they start to brown. Add the butter, let it melt, then add the parsley, shrimp, eggplant pulp, salt, paprika, thyme, and black pepper. Stir constantly until the shrimp begin to turn pink, about 5 minutes. When the shrimp look nearly done, stir in the bread crumbs. Lower the heat and continue to stir. When the ingredients are well combined, add the wine and stir again. Let this simmer for about 1 minute and remove from the stove.

3. Preheat the oven to 350°F. Line a 9 × 13-inch baking dish with the eggplant shells and fill with the stuffing mixture. Bake for 20 minutes and serve.

Serves 4

BAKED CUCUMBERS

ucumber is familiar as a raw vegetable eaten in salads, but did you know it tastes wonderful baked? This side dish is as pleasing to the eye as it is to the palate.

3 slices bacon, chopped
3 large cucumbers
2 tomatoes, peeled and chopped
1 small white onion, finely chopped
1 teaspoon salt
1 teaspoon freshly ground black pepper
½ cup bread crumbs, toasted under a broiler
1 tablespoon butter

1. In a heavy skillet, cook the chopped bacon over low heat, being careful not to fry, until golden in color. Briefly set aside.

2. Wash the cucumbers well, cut in half lengthwise, and scoop out the centers, leaving about a ¼-inch-thick shell. Roughly chop the cucumber pulp and combine it in a large mixing bowl with the tomatoes, onion, salt, and pepper. Preheat the oven to 350°F.

3. Place the skillet back on the stove over medium heat and add the cucumber mixture. Gently sauté the vegetables until they become limp, about 5 minutes. Add the bread crumbs and mix well. Remove the skillet from the stove and stuff the cucumber shells with the sautéed vegetables. Dot the tops with butter.

4. Arrange the cucumbers in a 9 × 13-inch baking dish and pour about ½ cup hot water around them. Bake for 30 minutes or until bubbly and serve immediately.

Serves 6

Vegetables & Side Dishes

CHAYOTES AU GRATIN

The chayote is a member of the squash family and is known in the Caribbean by several names: christophene, cho-cho, custard marrow, mirliton, and vegetable pear. A green, pear-shaped vegetable with an edible seed, it is most often boiled, halved, and filled with a stuffing that includes its own chopped pulp. This vegetable is originally from Mexico but is widely grown in tropical regions including the Caribbean and parts of Louisiana. Not only is it a delicious vegetable, but it is said to make an excellent substitute for apples in pie.

4   chayotes
½   pound smoked sausage, chopped (about 1¼ cups)
4   green onions, finely chopped (including green)
1   white onion, finely chopped
3   cloves garlic, minced
1   Scotch bonnet pepper, seeded and finely chopped
½   cup bread crumbs
½   cup milk
1   cup grated Gruyère cheese

1. Place the chayotes in a large saucepan or Dutch oven and add water to cover. Add salt if you like and bring to a brisk boil. Boil the chayotes until tender, 30 to 45 minutes, then cool and cut each in half lengthwise. Carefully scoop out the seeds and discard. Scoop out the pulp with a spoon, leaving a ¼-inch-thick shell. Coarsely chop the pulp and set aside for later use.

2. In a heavy skillet, brown the sausage. Add the green onions, white onion, garlic, and Scotch bonnet pepper and sauté until they are limp. Add the chayote pulp and continue to sauté. Add the bread crumbs and milk and stir well. When the mixture is well combined, remove from the stove.

3. Preheat the oven to 350°F. Arrange the chayote shells in a shallow baking dish. Make a layer of grated cheese in the bottom of each shell. Add a layer of the stuffing mixture and another layer of cheese. Repeat the layering until the shells are full. Bake the shells for 30 minutes or until the tops are bubbly. Serve immediately.

Serves 8

CREAMED CHAYOTES

This is a favorite way to prepare the chayote, or christophene, on the Spanish-speaking islands. The ingredients are simple and this dish is a perfect side to beef or chicken main courses.

4   **chayotes, halved lengthwise**

2   **tablespoons butter**

1   **white onion, finely chopped**

½   **cup grated Gruyère cheese**

    Bread crumbs, for topping

1. Boil the chayotes in salted water to cover for 20 minutes. Remove from the stove and drain. When cool enough to handle, roughly chop (including the shell) and set aside.

2. In a large skillet, melt the butter and sauté the onion until it becomes limp. Add the chayotes and stir well to combine. Cook for 5 minutes and remove from the stove. Preheat the oven to 350°F.

3. Add the grated cheese to the chayotes and stir well to combine. Transfer to a greased 9 × 13-inch baking dish, sprinkle with bread crumbs, and bake for 30 minutes.

Serves 4

Vegetables & Side Dishes

SMOTHERED CABBAGE *(Jamaica)*

Cabbage is a year-round crop in the Caribbean and is sold by the bundle in open-air markets where old ladies stand around and haggle about the price. In this recipe the cabbage is stewed with onion, carrots, and fresh thyme. It makes an excellent side dish for "Jerk" Chicken (page 98) or pork.

2 tablespoons butter

1 large white onion, finely chopped

3 quarts water

1 cup chicken stock

1 tablespoon salt

1 tablespoon freshly ground black pepper

3 sprigs fresh thyme

4 carrots, shredded

1 head green cabbage, shredded

In a large stockpot, melt the butter and sauté the onion until it is limp. Add the water, chicken stock, salt, pepper, and thyme and bring to a brisk boil over high heat. Add the carrots and boil for 10 minutes. Stir in the cabbage and bring the water back to a boil. Lower the heat, cover, and simmer, stirring occasionally, for about 1 hour or until the vegetables are tender and the water has evaporated. If the water is not evaporating, remove the cover for the last 15 minutes of cooking. Remove the thyme before serving.

Serve 4 to 6

Grenada

This food lover's paradise was discovered by Christopher Columbus on his third voyage, around 1498. Grenada is known as the spice island of the Caribbean and exports most of the world's cinnamon, nutmeg, saffron, clove, allspice, and bay leaf. It is said that the aroma of spice lingers in the lush tropical air. In addition to the spices, a bounty of native tropical fruits and vegetables are deliciously reflected in the island's cuisine. Rum punches are a big favorite, laced with the exotic flavor of nutmeg.

CREAMED CABBAGE *(Bahamas)*

Sinfully good, this rich vegetable dish is a wonderful complement to any light meat or fish entree. When boiling cabbage, take a tip from Caribbean cooks: add a splash of lime juice to the water. It prevents the cabbage from smelling up the house.

1   **head green cabbage, cut into wedges**

1   **tablespoon lime juice**

4   **strips bacon**

¼   **pound white Cheddar cheese, grated**

2   **tablespoons butter**

2   **tablespoons flour**

¾   **cup milk**

    Freshly ground black pepper to taste

    Dash cayenne pepper

    Salt to taste

1. Place the cabbage in a Dutch oven and cover with water. Add the lime juice and salt if desired and bring to a boil. Cook the cabbage for 1 hour or until the leaves become soft. Drain well.

2. Preheat the oven to 350°F and line a 9 × 13-inch baking dish with the strips of bacon. Add a layer of boiled cabbage and a layer of cheese. Repeat until all the cabbage and cheese have been used up.

3. In a heavy saucepan, melt the butter and stir in the flour. When well combined, add the milk, stirring constantly to prevent lumps. Add the black pepper, cayenne pepper, and salt and cook until slightly thickened. Pour the sauce over the top of the cabbage. Bake in the oven until the top is bubbly and brown, about 20 minutes.

Serves 6

Vegetables & Side Dishes

CARNIVAL CORN

For the most part, slaves were forced to maintain a vegetarian diet—meat was rarely given to them. As a result, corn became a staple, and they were very creative with ways of preparing it, as recipes such as this one demonstrate. We named our version for its colors: yellow, red, and green.

Anguilla

Christopher Columbus sighted this island on his second voyage and named it for its eellike shape. At the time of his arrival, the island was inhabited by fierce Carib Indians who were not exactly friendly. Needless to say, Columbus moved along. Anguilla was later settled by wild Irish settlers who had escaped white labor camps on other British islands. Today English is the official language, and the inhabitants are of African, Irish, Spanish, and French ancestry. Lobster is the king of the sea here, and highly seasoned conch and curried goat are specialities of the island.

4   strips lean bacon, chopped

½   cup (1 stick) butter

3   white onions, finely chopped

1   green pepper, seeded and finely chopped

1   cup chopped pimientos

4   cups fresh or canned corn

1½ teaspoons salt

1½ teaspoons freshly ground black pepper

In a Dutch oven, fry the bacon over moderate heat. When it begins to render fat, add the butter and melt it. Then add the onions and green pepper and sauté until they become limp. Stir in the pimientos, corn, salt, and pepper and cook, stirring, just long enough to heat the corn thoroughly, about 3 minutes. Serve immediately.

Serves 8

BROILED ARTICHOKE HEARTS AND TOMATOES

How could such a simple dish turn out to be so elegant? Quick and easy to make, it's the perfect complement to any heavy main course.

1   10-ounce package frozen artichoke hearts, thawed

1   tomato, sliced

2   tablespoons olive oil

¼   cup grated Parmesan cheese

1   tablespoon butter, melted

1   tablespoon chopped fresh basil

Salt to taste

Freshly ground black pepper to taste

Preheat the oven to broil. In a greased small baking dish, neatly arrange the artichokes and tomato slices. Sprinkle with the olive oil, cheese, butter, basil, salt, and pepper. Broil the vegetables until they sizzle and the cheese is lightly browned, about 10 minutes.

Serves 4

Vegetables & Side Dishes

SWEET PLANTAINS

Plantains are found on every island in the Caribbean and used in a number of ways. On the Spanish-speaking islands they are simply sliced and fried. Served with almost any main course—pork, beef, chicken, or fish—they are delicious and melt in your mouth.

2 very ripe sweet plantains

Oil for frying

Salt to taste

Freshly ground black pepper to taste

Peel and slice the plantains ¼ inch thick. Heat the oil in a deep fryer to 400°F and deep-fry the plantains until they are golden brown. Remove from the oil and drain on paper towels. Sprinkle with salt and pepper and serve immediately.

Serves 4

The Plantain

The plantain is a mainstay of the Caribbean diet. The fruit itself is not indigenous to the West Indies but was brought to the islands by missionaries and cultivated. Slave rations of food were not great but did include the plantain. Each slave received one to two bunches as a week's worth of provisions. They used plantains to make wine, boiled them like potatoes, and deep-fried them. The leaves were used to make paper and to steam foods.

FRIED GREEN PLANTAINS *(Puerto Rico)*

At Sugar Reef we call these delectable morsels Puerto Rican french fries, which comes pretty close to describing their actual taste. On the Spanish-speaking islands, they are called *tostones*. Green plantains are partly fried in hot oil, taken out of the pan, and flattened with a mallet. They are then returned to the oil and fried until golden brown and crispy.

2 green plantains

Oil for frying

Salt to taste

Freshly ground black pepper to taste

1. Peel and slice the plantains ¼ inch thick. Soak the slices in warm water for at least 40 minutes and drain.

2. Heat the oil in a deep fryer to 400°F. Fry the plantains for 1 to 2 minutes and remove from the oil. On a sturdy surface, flatten each slice with a heavy mallet. Pound it on both sides. Return to the hot oil and continue to fry until the plantains are golden brown. Drain on paper towels, salt and pepper as you like, and serve immediately.

Serves 4

Vegetables & Side Dishes

FOO FOO

Foo Foo is boiled green plantain that is mashed, lightly seasoned, and rolled into little balls. They are usually served with soups, stews, or callaloo as a starchy side dish.

4 **green plantains, skins on, ends trimmed**

1 **teaspoon salt**

1 **teaspoon freshly ground black pepper**

2 **tablespoons butter, softened**

1. In a large Dutch oven, bring 2 quarts of water to a brisk boil and add the plantains, salt, and pepper. Boil the plantains until the skins begin to loosen and the meat is tender, 45 minutes to 1 hour. Remove from the stove and drain.

2. Peel the plantains and mash them using a pestle and mortar. Dip the pestle in ice water to prevent sticking. When all of the meat is mashed and smooth, add the butter and stir well to combine. Using your hands, roll the plantain into little balls 2 to 3 inches in diameter.

Serves 4

St. Lucia

Many people feel that St. Lucia is the most beautiful island in the Caribbean. It has the world's only drive-through volcano (dormant, of course) and green sunsets. Its mountains peak higher than the Eiffel Tower, and sailors claim they are a majestic sight from the sea. Street vendors sell fresh hot sauces, baskets, and coal pots, heavy clay pots used in cooking foods over open fires. The islanders enjoy a bounty of fresh tropical fruits and vegetables, and celebrate their traditional festivals of La Rose and La Marguerite with flowers, dancing, special masses, and parades.

PAPAYA CASSEROLE

The papaya is considered both a fruit (when ripe) and a vegetable (when green). When green, it is used in stuffing and chutneys and in stews like this one. When ripe, it is used in drinks, desserts, and jams.

3 tablespoons butter

1 white onion, finely chopped

6 pounds green papayas, peeled, seeded, and chopped

4 tomatoes, peeled and chopped

1 teaspoon salt

1 teaspoon freshly ground black pepper

¼ cup bread crumbs

¼ cup grated Parmesan cheese

1. In a heavy skillet, melt the butter over medium heat and sauté the onion until limp. Add the papayas, tomatoes, salt, and pepper and simmer, covered, for about 15 minutes; stir occasionally. Uncover and continue to simmer until all the liquid has evaporated. Briefly set aside. Preheat the oven to 350°F.

2. In a small bowl, combine the bread crumbs with the cheese. Grease a baking dish and fill with the papaya mixture. Top with the bread crumbs and cheese and bake for 30 minutes or until bubbly.

Serves 6

Vegetables & Side Dishes

STUFFED PAW PAW

In this recipe the paw paw, or papaya, is stuffed with a delicious array of ingredients—fresh crabmeat, herbs, and vegetables—and lightly laced with white wine and brandy. The papayas you use should be semi-ripe and firm.

The Cayman Islands

Blackbeard made the Caymans his secret hideaway, and legends of hidden treasure abound to this day. Other early settlers included deserters from Oliver Cromwell's army, as well as a variety of Irish, Scottish, and English transplants, some of whom were shipwreck survivors. These famous founding fathers are celebrated every year during a Pirate Week Festival, when islanders dress up as rogues and wenches and search for that undiscovered treasure still hidden somewhere on the islands. The main tourist attraction is the post office in the village of Hell, where people flock to get postcards to the folks back home postmarked.

2   **papayas, halved lengthwise and seeded**
½   **pound white crabmeat**
½   **pound dark crabmeat**
¼   **cup (½ stick) butter**
½   **stalk celery, finely chopped**
1   **white onion, finely chopped**
1   **small red onion, finely chopped**
1   **carrot, finely chopped**
1   **green pepper, seeded and finely chopped**
1   **tomato, cubed**
1   **tablespoon Old Bay Seasoning**
½   **teaspoon salt**
½   **teaspoon dried thyme**
½   **teaspoon dried oregano**
½   **teaspoon freshly ground black pepper**
½   **teaspoon white pepper**
½   **cup white wine**
1   **tablespoon dry vermouth**
1   **tablespoon brandy**
½   **cup bread crumbs**

1. Scrape out the pulp from the papayas, leaving ¼-inch shells. Chop the pulp and set the shells aside for later use. Pick over the crabmeat to remove any bits of cartilage.

2. Preheat the oven to 350°F. In a Dutch oven, melt the butter over moderate heat and add the celery, onions, carrot, green pepper, tomato, chopped papaya, and crabmeat. Sauté for about 2 minutes. Add the Old Bay Seasoning, salt, thyme, oregano, black and white pepper, wine, vermouth, and brandy and stir until the mixture simmers, about 5 minutes. Add the bread crumbs to thicken. Stuff the papaya shells with the mixture and bake for 30 minutes.

Serves 4

147

PINEAPPLE SOUFFLÉ

A soufflé is a welcome change from the ordinary vegetable side dish to meats. The sweet yet delicate flavor of pineapple baked with eggs, flour, and butter is a pleasant contrast to the heavy flavor of most meats.

2½ cups crushed fresh pineapple (about 1 large)

3 eggs, beaten

¼ cup sugar

3 tablespoons flour

1½ tablespoons butter, melted

4 teaspoons lemon juice

Pinch of salt

1. Preheat the oven to 350°F. Place all the ingredients in a bowl and mix together well.

2. Spoon into a greased small baking dish or soufflé dish and bake for 45 minutes to 1 hour or until the soufflé has the consistency of soft pudding.

Serves 4

Vegetables & Side Dishes

GUYANESE POTATOES *(Guyana)*

Guyana is not an island but a Caribbean country on the north coast of South America. Like so many of the islands, it is a melting pot of cultures, and its cuisine reflects this fact. This recipe, of African–East Indian origins, is superb as a side for meat dishes, but in the Caribbean it is often eaten in roti bread as a lunchtime meal.

¼   cup vegetable oil

2   cloves garlic, minced

1   tablespoon dried whole rosemary

2   tablespoons curry powder

2   pounds potatoes, peeled and sliced

1   large ripe papaya or mango, peeled and cubed (or 1 cup pineapple chunks)

    Salt to taste

    Freshly ground black pepper to taste

1   to 1½ cups water

¼   cup (½ stick) butter, melted

1. Heat the oil in a Dutch oven or large skillet. Add the garlic and rosemary and sauté over moderate heat until the garlic begins to look crisp and golden. Strain the hot oil, removing the bits of garlic and rosemary, and pour back into the Dutch oven.

2. Reheat the oil and add the curry powder. Stir for 3 to 4 minutes, making sure that the curry and oil blend together. Add the potatoes, papaya, salt, pepper, and water. Stir until all the ingredients are combined and the water begins to boil. Lower the heat, cover, and simmer the potatoes, stirring occasionally, until they are tender, about 20 minutes.

3. Add the melted butter to the hot potatoes and serve immediately.

Serves 6

ISLAND YAMS *(Dominican Republic)*

This recipe was created by a dear friend from the Dominican Republic whom we affectionately call Tia (Spanish for "Aunt"). She has graced the kitchen at Sugar Reef from the very beginning and has inspired our menu tremendously. Although this side dish is excellent served with almost any main course, it is delicious enough to be a dessert.

6 to 8 yams or sweet potatoes, peeled and cubed

½ cup canned sweetened cream of coconut

½ cup dark rum

½ cup (1 stick) butter

¼ cup evaporated milk

Salt to taste

Freshly ground black pepper to taste

Place the yams in a Dutch oven and cover with water. Bring to a boil and cook the yams until soft, about 45 minutes. Drain and mash with a potato masher or large fork. Add the sweetened coconut milk, rum, butter, evaporated milk, salt, and pepper. Stir well until all the ingredients are combined and smooth. Serve immediately.

Serves 6

Vegetables & Side Dishes

YAM FRIES

Yams are a tropical root vegetable (actually a rhizome) and come in a variety of shapes and sizes, sometimes as big as 30 pounds! They are widely used in Caribbean cooking and have a pleasant nutty flavor. Often confused with the sweet potato, which belongs to an entirely different botanical family, yams can be cooked like any potato. These fries are a great change from ordinary french fries.

2 yams or sweet potatoes

Oil for frying

Salt to taste

Freshly ground black pepper to taste

1. Peel and slice the yams to make shoestring-size fries. Soak them in warm water for 30 minutes and drain. Do not soak for more than 30 minutes or you will not get crisp fries. Heat the oil in deep fryer to 400°F.

2. When the oil has reached the desired temperature, deep-fry the yams until they are golden brown and crispy. Drain on paper towels and sprinkle with salt and pepper. Serve immediately.

Serves 4

Dominica

This island is a big exporter of bananas, coconuts, grapefruit, limes, cocoa, and spices. It is also the home of the Jacquot and Sisserou parrots, two species found only on Dominica, which is a pretty amazing fact considering that the island is only 29 miles long and 15 miles wide. The native people speak a patois that is a mixture of French and English and their favorite food is mountain chicken, better known as frog.

CALABAZA PUMPKIN RICE

Calabaza is a green pumpkin or squash that should not be confused with our big orange Halloween pumpkin. It comes in a variety of shapes and sizes and is usually sold in Caribbean markets by the slice rather than whole. It has a delicate flavor that is very similar to butternut squash. Calabaza is a staple in the West Indies, where it is known by several names: abobora, crapaudback, Cuban squash, giraumon, and West Indian pumpkin.

¼ cup (½ stick) butter
2 cloves garlic, minced
1 white onion, finely chopped
4 green onions, finely chopped
1 Scotch bonnet pepper, seeded and finely chopped
3½ cups chicken stock
1 teaspoon salt
1 teaspoon freshly ground black pepper
1½ teaspoons ground allspice
2 sprigs fresh thyme
2 cups cubed and peeled calabaza pumpkin
1 cup water
1½ cups converted rice

1. In a Dutch oven, melt the butter and sauté the garlic, onion, green onions, and Scotch bonnet pepper until they are limp. Add 1 cup of the chicken stock and bring to a boil. Add the salt, pepper, allspice, thyme sprigs, and pumpkin. Lower the heat and simmer, covered, for about 1 hour, stirring occasionally. The pumpkin should be tender. Add more chicken stock if necessary.

2. Remove the thyme sprigs and add the remaining chicken stock and the water. Bring to a boil and add the rice. Stir well, lower the heat, and cover. Simmer for approximately 25 minutes or until the rice is fully cooked and all the liquid has been absorbed.

Serves 6

Vegetables & Side Dishes

RICE AND PEAS WITH COCONUT *(Jamaica)*

Often called the Jamaican Coat of Arms, this dish is a national favorite. Expatriates living in the United States dream of home when they smell the heady fragrance of spices, onion, and coconut simmering on the stove. In the islands, as in the South, *peas* is a generic term for any kind of dried bean. In this case, the choice is red kidney beans.

1   **pound dried red kidney beans, soaked overnight and drained**

2   **quarts water**

1   **quart chicken stock**

1   **cup coconut cream (page 10)**

2   **sprigs fresh thyme**

4   **allspice berries**

4   **green onions, finely chopped**

1   **small white onion, finely chopped**

2   **cloves garlic, minced**

1   **tablespoon freshly ground black pepper**

1   **tablespoon salt**

1   **Scotch bonnet pepper, whole (optional)**

2   **tablespoons canned sweetened cream of coconut (optional)**

4½   **cups long-grain rice**

1. In a large stockpot, combine the beans, water, chicken stock, and coconut cream. Bring to a brisk boil, stirring well. Lower the heat and cover the beans. Simmer for 1 to 2 hours, stirring occasionally, or until the beans are soft.

2. Add the thyme, allspice, green onions, white onion, garlic, black pepper, salt, Scotch bonnet pepper, and sweetened cream of coconut and stir well. Simmer for 3 to 4 minutes, add the rice, and stir again. There should be enough liquid in the pot to cover the rice by 1 inch. If not, add more water. Bring the mixture to a boil, lower the heat, and simmer, covered, until the rice is fully cooked, 20 to 30 minutes.

3. Remove the thyme sprigs and allspice berries. Serve while hot.

Serves 12

PIGEON PEAS AND RICE *(Barbados)*

When a Barbadian speaks of peas 'n' rice, he is referring to one bean only, the pigeon pea. Pigeon peas are also known as congo or gungo peas but not on this island. They are green or brownish green in color and the size of a small green pea but flatter. As on many other islands, this dish is a mainstay of the Bajan diet.

½   **pound ham hocks, hacked into pieces**

1   **small white onion, finely chopped**

4   **cups water**

    Bouquet garni (2 sprigs fresh thyme, 2 sprigs fresh marjoram, 1 bay leaf)

1   **teaspoon salt**

1   **teaspoon freshly ground black pepper**

1   **pound dried pigeon peas, soaked overnight and drained**

2   **cups long-grain rice**

In a large Dutch oven, brown the ham hocks on all sides until they are half cooked. Add the onion and sauté until limp. Add the water, bouquet garni, salt, and pepper and bring the mixture to a brisk boil over high heat. Add the peas and stir well to thoroughly combine all the ingredients. Bring the mixture back to a boil, lower the heat, and simmer the peas, covered, for 45 minutes. Stir in the rice, cover, and continue to simmer for another 20 minutes or until the water has been absorbed and the beans are tender. Remove the bouquet garni and serve.

Serves 8

Vegetables & Side Dishes

BLACK BEANS *(Cuba)*

Black beans are most popular on the Latin Caribbean islands. Other islands favor kidney beans, pigeon peas, or black-eyed peas. The preparation is simple and the results are superb. Coriander gives the beans their distinctive flavor.

Cuba

The Indians of the Caribbean told Columbus of a place they called Cibao (Cuba), which was an island nearby. He went to Cuba and proclaimed it to be Hispaniola and insisted that Cibao was a corruption of Cipango, Marco Polo's name for Japan. He was so fixated that he made his officers and crew take an oath that they, too, had no doubt that Cuba was a mainland and the beginning of the Indies. After this proclamation Columbus made no further efforts to explore the outlying regions and headed home for good, leaving the discovery of America, Central America, and Mexico to others.

1	white onion, finely chopped
2	cloves garlic, minced
1	green pepper, seeded and finely chopped
¼	cup olive oil
1	pound dried black beans, soaked overnight and drained
6	cups water
1½	cups chicken stock
¼	cup white wine
1	tablespoon salt
1	tablespoon freshly ground black pepper
	Bouquet garni (2 green onions, 2 sprigs fresh coriander, 2 sprigs fresh parsley, 1 bay leaf)

1. In a heavy Dutch oven, sauté the onion, garlic, and green pepper in the olive oil until they become limp. Add the beans, stir well, then add the water, chicken stock, wine, salt, pepper, and bouquet garni. Bring the mixture to a boil over moderate heat, stirring occasionally. Lower the heat and simmer the beans, covered, for 2 hours.

2. Uncover the beans and cook until the sauce thickens. Remove 1 cup of the beans and mash them until soupy. Return to the pot and stir in. Cook the beans for another 10 minutes and remove the bouquet garni. Serve with white rice.

Serves 8

MACARONI AND CHEESE

A Caribbean cookbook would not be complete without this dish, which is found on almost every island. Called *Macaronnes con Queso* on the Latin islands, it is a favorite starchy side dish and meatless main course.

2 tablespoons salt

1 tablespoon olive oil

½ pound elbow macaroni

¼ cup (½ stick) butter

½ cup flour

3 cups milk

1 egg yolk, beaten

1 cup grated Cheddar cheese

Fresh parsley leaves, for garnish

1. Fill a large stockpot with 3 quarts of water, add the salt and olive oil, and bring to a brisk boil. Add the macaroni and stir well. Cook until the pasta is tender, about 12 minutes. Drain in a colander and set aside.

2. Preheat the oven to 350°F. In a saucepan over moderate heat, melt the butter and stir in the flour until it is smooth. Add the milk and egg yolk and continue to stir. When the milk comes to a simmer, add ¾ cup of the grated cheese and stir to blend.

3. In a large baking dish, combine the macaroni with the cheese sauce until the pasta is completely covered. Top with the remaining cheese and bake for 30 minutes. Garnish with whole parsley leaves before serving.

Serves 6

Vegetables & Side Dishes

COU COU (Barbados)

Made of cornmeal, okra, water, salt and pepper, and butter, Cou Cou resembles a cornbread pudding. It is usually served steaming hot with a pat of butter, but some people like it with brown gravy when it accompanies the main course. Barbadians like Cou Cou with steamed or fried flying fish.

6 cups water

1 tablespoon salt

½ pound fresh okra, stem ends removed, finely chopped

1 teaspoon freshly ground black pepper

1 pound yellow cornmeal

2 tablespoons butter

1. Place 4 cups of the water and the salt in a heavy Dutch oven and bring to a brisk boil over high heat. Add the okra, reduce the heat, and simmer, covered, for 10 to 15 minutes or until the okra is tender.

2. Add the remaining water and return to a boil. Stir the pepper into the cornmeal and add it to the boiling water in a steady stream, stirring constantly with a wooden spoon. Cook the mixture, stirring, until it becomes stiff and smooth and moves away from the sides of the pot, about 12 minutes.

3. Place the Cou Cou in a serving bowl. Press and spread it out evenly to make a flat surface. This will shape the Cou Cou. Invert it onto a serving platter and top with the butter. Serve immediately.

Serves 4 to 6

Desserts
&
Breads

LIME MOUSSE

Light and refreshing, this chilled dessert is zesty with the flavor of fresh lime. It's a refreshing contrast after any spicy main course.

3½ cups water

¾ cup flour

¾ cup cornstarch

¼ teaspoon salt

3 cups sugar

9 eggs, separated

3 tablespoons grated lime rind

½ teaspoon vanilla extract

Juice of 3 limes

3 tablespoons butter

½ cup heavy cream

Shredded coconut, for garnish

Lime slices, for garnish

1. In a heavy saucepan, heat the water until hot but not boiling. Slowly stir in the flour, cornstarch, salt, and sugar. Continue to stir until the mixture starts to thicken. In a bowl, combine the egg yolks, lime rind, and vanilla. Stir a spoonful of the hot liquid into the egg yolks to warm them, then slowly add the yolks to the saucepan, stirring constantly. Add the lime juice, butter, and cream and continue to stir for another 2 minutes. Remove the pan from the stove and stir well to prevent the pudding from sticking to the bottom. Cover and set aside briefly.

2. In a large bowl, beat the egg whites with a whisk until very stiff. Fold into the pudding until completely incorporated. Divide the mousse among 6 wineglasses. Garnish each with coconut and a lime slice. Let cool to room temperature, then refrigerate for at least 1 hour.

Serves 6

Desserts & Breads

MANGO MOUSSE

Versatile and popular in Caribbean cooking, the mango lends itself well to an array of recipes. This light and fluffy mousse, garnished with fresh mint, is a beautiful way to end a meal.

4 to 5 very ripe 1-pound mangoes, peeled and pitted

Juice of 2 limes

¼ cup superfine sugar

1 envelope unflavored gelatin, dissolved in 2 tablespoons hot water

2 egg whites, beaten

¼ teaspoon salt

¾ cup heavy cream

Fresh mint leaves, for garnish

1. In a food processor, puree the mangoes. Add the lime juice, sugar, and gelatin and briefly process to combine.

2. In a large bowl, combine the egg whites with the salt and beat until stiff enough to hold peaks. In a separate large bowl, beat the cream until stiff.

3. Gently fold the mango puree into the egg whites, then fold the whipped cream into the mousse. Pour into one large or 8 individual serving bowls and refrigerate until the mousse is firm, about 3 hours. Garnish with fresh mint leaves.

Serves 8

The Passion Fruit

The passion fruit was named for the sufferings of Christ, not for the promise of sensual delight. Remember this the next time you think of sneaking a little Caribbean passion fruit onto the menu of your next romantic interlude. The recipes in this book do not call for this tropical fruit because of the difficulty of locating it in most American markets. If you do find a ripe passion fruit, try substituting it for the papaya or mango in any recipe.

BLANCMANGE *(Haiti)*

This light, mousselike dessert, rich with coconut flavor, is a traditional Haitian recipe. It's a perfect ending to any meal, but is especially suitable after a heavy entree.

1½ cups coconut cream (page 10)

1½ cups evaporated milk

1 14-ounce can sweetened condensed milk

2 envelopes unflavored gelatin, dissolved in ¼ cup hot water

½ cup grated coconut

1 tablespoon sugar

1. In a saucepan over moderate heat, bring the coconut cream, evaporated milk, condensed milk, and gelatin to a boil, stirring constantly. Immediately remove the saucepan from the heat and pour the mixture into a 6-cup mold or serving dish. Let the pudding cool to room temperature, then refrigerate for at least 4 hours.

2. Preheat the oven to broil. Place the grated coconut on a flat baking pan or cookie sheet and spread out thinly. Sprinkle the coconut with the sugar and place the pan under the broiler to toast the flakes for 5 to 10 minutes or until golden brown. (Omit the sugar if you use packaged sweetened coconut.) Remove the coconut from the broiler and briefly set aside to cool. Just before serving, top the pudding with the toasted coconut.

Serves 8

Desserts & Breads

FLOATING ISLANDS *(Jamaica)*

This unusual dessert is time-consuming to make but well worth the effort. The "islands" are spoonfuls of whipped custard, guava, and whipped cream.

4 eggs, separated
¼ cup sugar
1¾ cup light cream
¼ cup guava jelly
½ cup heavy cream
2 tablespoons confectioner's sugar
¼ cup dark rum

1. In a large bowl, beat the egg yolks and sugar with a wire whisk until they start to thicken, about 3 minutes. Slowly add the light cream, whisking continuously for at least 1 minute. Pour into a heavy saucepan and bring to a simmer over low heat. Cook, stirring constantly, until the mixture thickens and coats a spoon, about 10 minutes. Be careful not to allow it to reach the boiling point. Remove the pudding from the stove, let it cool to room temperature, then refrigerate until completely chilled and firm.

2. When you are nearly ready to serve the dessert, melt the guava jelly in a small saucepan over low heat and set aside. In a large bowl, beat the egg whites until stiff, then slowly whip in the melted jelly.

3. In a chilled mixing bowl, beat the heavy cream until it begins to thicken, then slowly whisk in the confectioner's sugar and rum.

4. Remove the pudding from the refrigerator and make floating islands by spooning the guava–egg white mixture on top, spacing the islands about an inch apart. Serve on individual dessert plates and place a large spoonful of the whipped cream on the side.

Serves 6

TIA'S FABULOUS RICE PUDDING *(Dominican Republic)*

Tia is in charge of our daytime crew at Sugar Reef and is responsible for many of the recipes in this book. This is one of her family recipes from the Dominican Republic.

¾ cup long-grain rice
1 teaspoon salt
1 quart milk
¾ cup sugar
1 teaspoon ground nutmeg
1 teaspoon ground cinnamon
1 teaspoon vanilla extract
¾ cup dark raisins
   Whipped cream, for garnish
   Shredded coconut or whole maraschino cherries, for garnish

1. Preheat the oven to 300°F. In a large baking dish, combine the rice, salt, milk, sugar, nutmeg, cinnamon, and vanilla and stir well. Bake for 1½ hours, stirring the pudding every 30 minutes during baking. Remove the dish from the oven and stir in the raisins. Bake the pudding for another 20 minutes.

2. Cool on a rack to room temperature, then refrigerate until chilled. Or, if you prefer, serve it warm with fresh whipped cream. Garnish with shredded coconut or a cherry.

Serves 4 to 6

Desserts & Breads

BANANA PUDDING WITH LEMON SAUCE

This all-fruit pudding is made without the assistance of milk. The topping is a delightfully sweet and zesty lemon sauce.

16   ripe bananas
½   cup sugar
1   teaspoon lemon juice
1   egg, well beaten
     Butter
     Lemon slices, for garnish

LEMON SAUCE:
2   cups water
½   cup sugar
1   tablespoon flour
2   tablespoons grated lemon rind
     Juice of 1 lemon
1   egg, lightly beaten
     Lemon slices, for garnish

1. Preheat the oven to 350°F. In a large bowl, mash the bananas well. Add the sugar, lemon juice, and egg, stirring well, and pour into a greased small baking dish. Bake for 1 hour or until a toothpick inserted in the center comes out clean.

2. While the pudding is baking, make the Lemon Sauce. Bring the water to a boil in a saucepan. In a small bowl, combine the sugar and flour and slowly add to the boiling water, stirring constantly. Lower the flame and simmer, stirring, until the mixture begins to thicken. Mix the lemon rind and lemon juice into the egg and add to the saucepan, stirring constantly until smooth and thick, about 3 minutes. Serve immediately with the hot banana pudding and garnish each serving with a slice of lemon.

Serves 8

BANANAS WITH RUM CUSTARD

This is such an easy recipe, and it perfectly teams up dark Caribbean rum with fresh bananas. Don't be surprised if your guests ask for seconds.

4 egg yolks, beaten
2 cups heavy cream
¼ cup sugar
¼ teaspoon salt
2 tablespoons dark rum
1 teaspoon vanilla extract
6 ripe bananas, peeled and sliced in half lengthwise
Ground nutmeg, for garnish

1. In a double boiler, combine the egg yolks, cream, sugar, and salt and stir until thoroughly blended. Over simmering water, heat the mixture, stirring continuously, until it coats the spoon and starts to thicken. Remove the double boiler from the stove and strain the custard into a heatproof bowl. Stir in the rum and vanilla.

2. Arrange the bananas on individual serving plates and top with the custard while it is still warm. Lightly sprinkle with nutmeg and serve immediately.

Serves 6

Desserts & Breads

CHOCOLATE FLAN

Flan is as popular on the Spanish-speaking islands as it is in Spain, where it originated. The addition of chocolate and rum gives yet another dimension to this delectable dessert.

8 eggs
1 12-ounce can evaporated milk
1½ cups milk
1 cup plus 2 tablespoons sugar
1 teaspoon vanilla extract
6 tablespoons (3 ounces) dark rum
3 ounces (squares) semisweet chocolate, melted

1. Place the eggs, evaporated milk, whole milk, 2 tablespoons of the sugar, and the vanilla and rum in a blender and blend on high for about 3 minutes. Slowly add the melted chocolate and blend for another 2 minutes.

2. Preheat the oven to 350°F. In a small heavy saucepan, melt the remaining 1 cup of sugar, stirring constantly until it dissolves. Keep stirring until the sugar begins to caramelize. Pour the melted sugar into a 9-inch cake pan and spread evenly over the bottom.

3. Pour the blender mixture into the pan and place the pan in a larger pan with 1 inch of hot water. Bake for 30 minutes or until the custard is firm. Cool to room temperature on a rack, then refrigerate until completely chilled. To serve, run a spatula around the sides of the pan and invert onto a serving plate.

Serves 8 to 10

PINEAPPLE FLUFF

Just about everyone knows what a pineapple tastes like, so there is little need for introduction. As always, we recommend using a fresh one because the taste is superior, but for this recipe the canned fruit will also work.

¼ cup (½ stick) butter, softened

¼ cup sugar

2 eggs, separated

½ cup graham cracker crumbs

1 cup crushed and drained pineapple

Juice of 1 lime

½ teaspoon ground cinnamon

Whipped cream, for garnish

1. Preheat the oven to 300°F. In a large bowl, cream the butter and sugar until fluffy. Add the egg yolks and beat until well blended. Add the graham cracker crumbs, pineapple, lime juice, and cinnamon and mix well to combine the ingredients.

2. In a separate bowl, whip the egg whites until foamy and fold into the pineapple mixture. Pour into a greased 9 × 13-inch baking dish and bake for 30 minutes or until the top is lightly browned. Serve cold or hot, topped with whipped cream.

Serves 4

Desserts & Breads

BANANAS FLAMBÉ

The banana was among one of the first plants to be cultivated. Due to its popularity, it quickly spread from Southeast Asia throughout the world, including Africa and later to the Caribbean. For this recipe, look for bananas with brown speckles on the peel, which are a sign of ripeness. To add drama to a special meal, dim the lights and flambé the bananas at the table over a portable burner.

½   cup (1 stick) butter
½   cup brown sugar
4   ripe bananas, peeled and quartered
½   cup dark rum
1   pint vanilla ice cream

In a heavy skillet over moderate heat, melt the butter and add the brown sugar. Stir constantly until the sugar and butter combine and start to bubble. Add the bananas and simmer for 10 to 15 minutes. Add the rum and ignite. Let it burn briefly, smother the flame, and cook for another 5 minutes. Put scoops of vanilla ice cream in individual serving bowls and top with the bananas. Serve immediately.

Serves 4

LEMON AND GINGER SORBET

Ginger is a key ingredient in island cooking. It is considered a guard against disease and an aid in the digestion of food, which is why it is prevalent in desserts. Teamed with the zest of lemon and the rich flavor of rum, it makes a light and refreshing sorbet.

2	cups water
1¼	cups sugar
3	tablespoons grated fresh ginger
1	cup lemon juice
2	teaspoons grated lemon rind
¼	cup dark rum
4	lemon slices coated with brown sugar, for garnish

1. In a heavy saucepan, combine the water, sugar, and ginger and bring to a brisk boil, stirring well. Add the lemon juice and rind and simmer, stirring, for about 4 minutes. Remove the saucepan from the heat and pour its contents into freezer trays. Freeze until solid.

2. When the sorbet is completely frozen, scoop it out into a blender. Blend the sorbet until it becomes slushy. Add the rum and quickly blend again for about 15 seconds. Pour into individual serving dishes and place them in the freezer to firm up. The sorbet will not freeze completely because of the alcohol. It should be smooth. Garnish each serving with a lemon slice that has been dipped in brown sugar.

Serves 4

Desserts & Breads

FRUIT COMPOTE *(Cuba)*

For this recipe we prefer fresh fruit for a light, less sweet dessert. However, in Cuba canned fruit is often used because the heavy sugar syrup easily covers the cheese. The Cubans ladle the compote over a slab of cream cheese, but you may prefer something lighter, like farmer cheese or ricotta.

Tropical Fruits

More than 3,000 species of delectable fruits are native to the Caribbean. Unfortunately, only a few could be included in our recipes because most are unavailable in America. There is, for example, the mamey, a Santo Domingo version of the apricot, or the Malay apple, which is shaped like a pear, or a Jamaican plum called the mamoncillo. Then there is the Bluggoe fig, which is a petite purple banana used as a vegetable, the breadfruit, which, yes, looks like bread, the shiny and yellow carambola, shaped like a perfect five-pointed star, and passion fruit, which tastes like lemon, pineapple, and guava all rolled into one tearshaped bulb. *(Continued on page 173.)*

½ cup (1 stick) unsalted butter

½ cup sugar

1 ripe guava, peeled, seeded, and sliced (optional)

1 ripe mango, peeled, pitted, and sliced

1 ripe papaya, peeled, seeded, and sliced

2 tablespoons (1 ounce) dark rum

2 8-ounce packages cream cheese (or farmer cheese)

Shredded coconut, for garnish

1. In a heavy saucepan, melt the butter over medium heat and add the sugar. Stir constantly until the sugar melts, 5 to 10 minutes. Lower the heat and add the guava, mango, and papaya slices. Stir well to coat with the butter and sugar. Let the fruit simmer, stirring occasionally, for about 15 minutes or until the sauce begins to thicken. Add the rum and simmer another 5 to 10 minutes.

2. Remove the saucepan from the stove and let the fruit cool to room temperature. Place a portion of cheese on 8 individual plates. Stir the compote thoroughly and divide equally among the plates, spooning on top of the cheese. Sprinkle each serving with shredded coconut.

Serves 8

MANGO SNOW

Mangoes are native to India and made their way to Africa and then the Caribbean. According to one story, the Arawak Indians overtook an unsuspecting French ship anchored off one of the islands. It was full of mangoes, which were immediately taken ashore for a big celebration. Everyone was awarded the delectable fruit as a prize, and the seeds were planted and cultivated. Thus the mango became a staple of the Caribbean diet. Sweet, juicy, and fragrant, a ripe mango makes a wonderful dessert in itself. Added to vanilla ice cream, it is exquisite.

2   very ripe mangoes, peeled, pitted, and sliced

1   quart vanilla ice cream

Let the ice cream stand at room temperature for 15 to 20 minutes to soften. Scoop into a large bowl and add the mango slices. Stir well to thoroughly combine the fruit and ice cream. Serve immediately or cover and place in the freezer until ready to serve. Do not make too far in advance because the ice cream should not refreeze completely.

Serves 8

Desserts & Breads

MANGO AND PINEAPPLE PIE

In the old days mangoes and pineapples were considered a luxury and were not available to everyone. Today both are major crops for the Caribbean and are sold year round in local markets, affordable to all.

More Tropical Fruits

The guanabana, or soursop, is a fruit with a spiky green skin, and the sweetsop, a relative of the soursop, is shaped like a heart and textured like a pine cone. The ackee is a large black seed with delicious edible flesh that looks like scrambled eggs and is also called vegetable brains. The ortanique is a mixup between an orange and a tangerine, and the ugli fruit is another version of mixed citrus, this time tangerine and grapefruit (it is really ugly on the outside but really tasty on the inside). The acerola is a West Indian cherry used for wines, and the dunk fruit is popular with children. These are just a few of the exotic fruits found in the Caribbean!

1 large pineapple, peeled and sliced in ¼-inch cubes

2 large ripe mangoes, peeled, pitted, and cut in long strips

½ cup brown sugar

1 teaspoon ground cinnamon

1 teaspoon ground nutmeg

1 teaspoon vanilla extract

2½ cups water

2 teaspoons cornstarch stirred into 2 tablespoons water

Pastry for 2-crust pie

¼ cup confectioner's sugar

1. In a large heavy saucepan, combine the pineapple, mangoes, brown sugar, cinnamon, nutmeg, vanilla, and water. Place over medium heat and cook, stirring constantly, for 10 to 15 minutes or until the fruit gets soft. Add the cornstarch and continue to stir until the mixture thickens, about 10 minutes.

2. Preheat the oven to 375°F. Line a 9-inch pie pan with pastry and fill with the fruit. Cover with the top pastry, seal the edges, and make some slits in the top.

3. Bake for 30 minutes or until the crust is golden brown. Allow the pie to cool and sprinkle the top with the confectioner's sugar.

Serves 8

LIME PIE

Limes are plentiful throughout the Caribbean year round and form an integral part of the cuisine. The most common variety is the same as Florida's Key lime. The flavor is more tart than the Persian lime found in most U.S. markets. By all means, use Key limes if you can get them.

4 egg yolks, beaten

1 14-ounce can sweetened condensed milk

½ cup lime juice

1 egg white, beaten until stiff

1 9-inch pie shell, baked

Whipped cream, for garnish

Grated lime rind, for garnish

1. Preheat the oven to 350°F. In a large bowl, mix the egg yolks with the condensed milk. Add the lime juice and stir well. When the mixture starts to combine, fold in the egg white and pour into the pie shell.

2. Bake the pie for 20 minutes or until the filling has a cheesecake consistency. Serve warm or cold, topped with whipped cream and garnished with grated lime rind.

Serves 8

Desserts & Breads

RUM CAKE *(Curaçao)*

his festive cake is served on holidays in the Dutch islands. Serve it plain as a coffee cake or with homemade ice cream as a dessert.

Curaçao

Curaçao has easily been the most accommodating country for political refugees of the past few centuries. It was a major refuge for Jews escaping the Spanish Inquisition and until 1825 had the largest Jewish community in the Americas. The oldest Jewish cemetery (1659) in the Western Hemisphere is on the island, as well as the oldest synagogue (1732). Curaçao was also important to those fighting for the independence of Latin America and provided protection for the famous liberator Simón Bolívar. Ships and people have benefited from the island's safe harbor, the seventh largest and second busiest port in the world.

½ cup butter, softened

1 cup sugar

4 eggs

2 tablespoons lime juice

3 to 4 tablespoons dark rum

1 tablespoon grated lime rind

1 cup flour

1½ teaspoons baking powder

Confectioner's sugar, for garnish

1. Preheat the oven to 350°F. In a large bowl, cream the butter and sugar until fluffy. Beat in the eggs, one at a time, then the lime juice, rum, and lime rind. Sift the flour and baking powder together and add to the mixture a spoonful at a time, mixing in well.

2. Grease an 8-inch Bundt cake pan and lightly flour it. Pour in the batter and bake for 1 hour or until a toothpick inserted in the center comes out clean. Sprinkle the top with powdered sugar before serving.

Serves 10 to 12

MAMA PEABODY'S FAMOUS ESPRESSO CHOCOLATE TORTE

 The ultimate in chocolate desserts.

12 **ounces bittersweet chocolate**

12 **ounces semisweet chocolate**

½ **cup (1 stick) butter**

1 **cup brewed espresso coffee**

1 **cup sugar**

12 **eggs, 6 separated**

1 **tablespoon confectioner's sugar**

Confectioner's sugar, for garnish

Orange slices, for garnish

1. Preheat the oven to 325°F. In a large saucepan over low heat, melt the chocolate, butter, espresso, and sugar, stirring constantly. When the chocolate has completely melted and the ingredients have combined, transfer the mixture to a large bowl. In a separate bowl, beat the 6 whole eggs with the 6 egg yolks. Stir in a little of the chocolate mixture to warm the eggs, then add them to the chocolate. Briefly set aside.

2. In a separate large bowl, beat the remaining egg whites until almost stiff. Slowly add the confectioner's sugar and continue to beat until stiff. Fold into the chocolate mixture until thoroughly combined. Pour into a greased 9-inch springform pan.

3. Bake the torte for 35 minutes or until it has risen. Test with a knife—the center should be slightly moist. Let the torte cool for 30 minutes and transfer to a cake plate. Dust the top with confectioner's sugar, if you like, and garnish each serving with an orange slice.

Serves 10

Desserts & Breads

BANANA BREAD

Bananas are the world's favorite fruit. High in vitamins and minerals, they can be prepared in a variety of ways. One of our favorites is banana bread right out of the oven, topped with butter. As a breakfast treat, it sure beats floating banana slices in milk and cereal.

1   cup flour
2   teaspoons baking powder
1   teaspoon ground nutmeg
½   teaspoon salt
¾   cup superfine sugar
½   cup (1 stick) softened butter
1   egg, beaten
½   teaspoon vanilla extract
2   large ripe bananas, peeled and mashed
¼   cup dark raisins
½   cup chopped pecans

1. Preheat the oven to 350°F. Sift together the flour, baking powder, nutmeg, and salt. In a large bowl, cream the sugar and butter until light and fluffy, then add the beaten egg and vanilla. Mix thoroughly. Slowly add the flour mixture, a few spoonfuls at a time, mixing well after each addition. Stir in the mashed bananas, combine thoroughly, then add the raisins and nuts.

2. Pour the dough into a greased 9 × 5-inch loaf pan and distribute it evenly. Bake for 1 hour or until a toothpick inserted in the center comes out clean. Cool the bread on a wire rack before removing it from the pan.

Yield: 1 loaf

SWEET CASSAVA BREAD

Arawak Indians taught early settlers of the Caribbean many of the uses of cassava, the long, tuber-shaped root of the cassava plant. Also known as yuca or yucca, it has a dark, tough bark and hard, white flesh. There are two varieties of cassava, bitter and sweet. The bitter, reputed to be poisonous until cooked, is used primarily in commercially made products such as tapioca. The sweet is used in homemade treats like this one, which is widely known as Bammie. Lightly toasted with butter and topped with fresh jam, it is a breakfast favorite and is often eaten at tea time.

2   cups grated cassava

1   cup grated coconut

1   teaspoon salt

¼   cup brown sugar

Spread the grated cassava between double thicknesses of paper towels and press to remove excess moisture. In a large bowl, thoroughly mix all the ingredients together. Heat a medium iron skillet over high heat, add the mixture to the pan, and spread it out evenly. Cook over high heat for about 2 minutes, then turn like a pancake. Cook the other side until golden brown. Serve while hot with jam or preserves.

Serves 6

Desserts & Breads

CORNMEAL PONE

This is the Caribbean version of cornbread, but what a difference! It is wonderful with soups and stews. Or eat it warm, just from the oven, slathered with lots of butter.

1 cup yellow cornmeal
¼ cup dark raisins
1 teaspoon salt
½ cup sugar
2 cups grated fresh coconut
½ pound pumpkin, peeled and grated
2 tablespoons butter, melted
½ cup milk

1. Preheat the oven to 350°F. In a large bowl, combine the cornmeal, raisins, salt, sugar, coconut, and pumpkin. Stir in the melted butter, then add up to ½ cup milk. The dough should be fairly stiff. Beat with a wooden spoon until all the ingredients have combined.

2. Spread the dough in a greased 9 × 13-inch baking pan and bake for 30 minutes or until a toothpick inserted in the center comes out clean.

Serves 6

Short'nin' Bread
Afro-Garib song

Put on the skillet. Put on the pan.
Ma-ma's gonna make a little short'nin' bread
Ma-ma's little baby loves short'nin', shortning.
Ma-ma's little baby loves short'ning bread.

CONKIES *(Barbados)*

This sweet was invented by the first inhabitants of the Caribbean, the Arawak Indians. A combination of pumpkin, coconut, cornmeal, and brown sugar is wrapped in banana leaves and steamed. In Barbados it is traditionally served on Independence Day, November 30.

2   cups yellow cornmeal

½   cup flour

     Grated meat of 1 coconut

1   calabaza pumpkin (about ¾ pound), peeled and grated

1   yam, peeled and grated

½   cup dark raisins

¾   cup brown sugar

¼   cup white sugar

1   teaspoon salt

1   teaspoon ground nutmeg

1   teaspoon ground cinnamon

1   teaspoon almond extract

¾   cup butter, melted

1   cup milk (optional)

     Banana leaves (or foil)

1. In a large bowl, combine the cornmeal, flour, coconut, pumpkin, yam, raisins, brown sugar, white sugar, salt, nutmeg, cinnamon, and almond extract. Mix together well and add the butter to form a smooth dough. If the dough is dry and crumbly, add up to 1 cup milk.

2. Cut the banana leaves or foil into 6-inch squares. In the center of each square, place 2 to 3 tablespoons of the conkie dough. Fold together the edges to form a packet and tie with string. Steam the conkies over boiling water in a steamer for 1 hour. Unwrap and serve.

Serves 4 to 6

Desserts & Breads

WEST INDIAN BANANA FRITTERS

This versatile recipe is great for breakfast, served in place of the usual muffin. Or accompany the warm fritters with ice cream or sorbet for an unusual dessert.

4 very ripe bananas, peeled
½ cup flour
2 eggs, lightly beaten
2 tablespoons sugar
　 Pinch of salt
　 Oil for deep frying
　 Confectioner's sugar

1. In a large bowl, mash the bananas well. Add the flour, eggs, sugar, and salt and beat to form a stiffish dough.

2. Preheat the oil to 400°F in a deep fryer. Drop the dough by the spoonful into the hot oil and fry until golden brown, 3 to 5 minutes. Drain on paper towels and sprinkle with confectioner's sugar. Serve immediately.

Serves 6

The Banana

Bananas first grew in southern Asia and quickly spread to other areas of the world. The plant grows from bulbs and is formed by large, tough leaves that wrap around and around until they create a strong stalk, almost as strong as a woody tree. The banana was introduced in the Caribbean by Spanish missionaries who found them on the Canary Islands. Not only was the fruit incorporated into Caribbean cooking, but the strong leaves were used to wrap and steam foods.

BAKES *(Trinidad)*

These flat, round cakes are made simply with flour, sugar, salt, and baking powder. Fried to golden perfection, they are served as bread with lunch or dinner, or toasted for breakfast with jam.

1½ cups flour
  1 teaspoon baking powder
  1 teaspoon salt
  1 tablespoon butter
  2 teaspoons sugar
  ¼ cup ice water
     Oil for frying

1. Sift together the flour, baking powder, and salt. In a large bowl, cream the butter and sugar until smooth. Add the sifted ingredients and combine until crumbly. Add the cold water and beat to form a dough.

2. Knead the dough lightly on a surface dusted with flour. Pull off pieces of dough and roll into walnut-size balls. Flatten the balls to about ½ inch thick.

3. In a heavy skillet, heat ½ inch of oil. Fry the dough, 5 pieces at a time, until golden brown, about 3 minutes on each side. Drain on paper towels and serve immediately.

Yield: About 12 bakes

Desserts & Breads

KORISHA'S DALPOORI *(Trinidad)*

Our good friend Everold Hussein, a native of Trinidad, shared this family recipe for a variation of *roti* bread. East Indians brought *roti* to the Caribbean in the late nineteenth century. Often described as Indian bread, it is made by rolling dough into flat, round pieces and baking on a cast-iron griddle called a *tawa*. There are all kinds of *roti*, but a favorite of Trinidadians is *dalpoori*, which is stuffed with spiced, ground split peas (*dal*). Eaten with curries to soak up the sauce, it makes a great lunch or evening sandwich. The *dalpoori* is topped with curried potatoes and meat or shrimp, splashed with hot sauce, and folded over on all four sides.

SPLIT PEA FILLING:
- 1 cup dried yellow split peas
- ½ teaspoon turmeric
- ¼ teaspoon ground cumin
- ¼ teaspoon garlic powder

DOUGH:
- 2 cups flour
- 2 teaspoons baking powder
- ½ teaspoon salt
- ½ teaspoon sugar
- 1 tablespoon shortening
- Water (about ¼ cup)

1. In a large saucepan, bring 2 cups salted water to a boil. Add the split peas and turmeric and stir. Boil the peas for 30 minutes or until they are tender but not mushy. Drain off the water and transfer the peas to a blender or food processor. Add the cumin and garlic powder and process until almost smooth—there should still be some texture. Set aside while mixing the dough.

2. Stir the flour, baking powder, salt, and sugar together, cut in the shortening, and add enough water to form a soft dough. Let stand, covered, for about 1 hour.

3. Divide the dough into 4 portions and flatten each one slightly. Make a depression in the center and put in the split pea filling. Bring all the sides together and close over the top to make a ball with the filling inside. Lightly coat each ball of dough with flour and let them stand, covered with a cloth, for about 15 minutes.

4. Flatten each ball of dough and roll out to a 5-inch circle about ¼ inch thick. Heat an ungreased cast-iron griddle or skillet until hot enough to make a drop of cold water sizzle. Place the *roti* on the griddle and let them cook for about 2 minutes or until the bottom starts to have brown spots. Turn and let the other side cook. Brush the top side with melted butter and, when the second side is done, turn it over and brush it with butter also. Transfer the roti to a warm plate and keep covered. They are best when served hot.

Serves 4

Sauces

SAUCE TI-MALICE

 Every island has several varieties of hot sauce. This is one of our favorites from the isle of Haiti. The name speaks for itself.

10 large ripe tomatoes, peeled and quartered	3 tablespoons brown sugar
3 white onions, quartered	1 tablespoon salt
4 Scotch bonnet peppers, seeded	2 cups malt vinegar

Puree the tomatoes, onions, and Scotch bonnet peppers in a food processor. Transfer to a large saucepan and add the brown sugar, salt, and vinegar; stir well to combine. Cook the sauce over moderate heat, stirring occasionally, until it begins to boil. Lower the heat and simmer the sauce for 20 minutes, continuing to stir occasionally. Bottle the sauce in hot sterilized jars.

Yield: 3 pints

SAUCE PIQUANTE

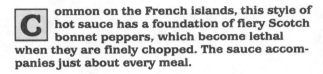 **C**ommon on the French islands, this style of hot sauce has a foundation of fiery Scotch bonnet peppers, which become lethal when they are finely chopped. The sauce accompanies just about every meal.

1 cup finely chopped white onion	¾ cup boiling water
	Juice of 1 lime
¼ cup finely chopped green onion	1 teaspoon salt
2 cloves garlic, minced	1 teaspoon freshly ground black pepper
2 Scotch bonnet peppers, seeded and finely chopped	2 tablespoons dried thyme

In a heatproof bowl, combine the white onion, green onion, garlic, and Scotch bonnet peppers and pour the boiling water on top. Stir in the lime juice, salt, black pepper, and thyme. Let the sauce cool at room temperature for at least 1 hour before serving.

Yield: 2 cups

Sauces

JACKIE'S HOT SAUCE

J ackie, a Trinidadian friend we met on a trip to Barbados, generously gave us this family recipe for Scotch bonnet pepper sauce. What makes it so special and flavorful is the combination of green papaya with the tartness of vinegar and lime and the bite of the hot pepper. This sauce gets better with age and tastes great on just about everything.

1	green papaya, peeled, seeded and roughly chopped		Grated rind of 1 lime
10	Scotch bonnet peppers, seeded	½	cup lime juice
2	onions, quartered	1½	cups malt vinegar
3	cloves garlic	1	teaspoon salt
		¼	cup prepared yellow mustard

Puree the papaya, Scotch bonnet peppers, onions, garlic, lime rind, and lime juice in a food processor. Transfer to a medium saucepan and stir in the vinegar, salt, and mustard. Simmer the mixture over low heat for 20 minutes, stirring occasionally. Bottle the sauce in hot sterilized jars.

Yield: 2 pints

WEST INDIAN MARINADE

T his flavorful marinade is equally good on meats, fish, and chicken. It is even easier to make if all the chopping is done in a food processor. At Sugar Reef we like to make it in large quantities and keep it in the refrigerator, ready for use. It can be stored for at least a week.

1	white onion, finely chopped	½	cup chicken stock
1	green pepper, seeded and finely chopped	½	cup white wine vinegar
1	Scotch bonnet pepper, seeded and finely chopped		Juice of 1 lime
		1	teaspoon sweet paprika
2	cloves garlic, minced	1	teaspoon dried oregano
1	teaspoon salt	2	sprigs fresh coriander, finely chopped
1	teaspoon freshly ground black pepper	2	sprigs fresh parsley, finely chopped

In a large bowl, combine all the ingredients to form a paste. Cover and refrigerate.

Yield: About 2½ cups

SALSA AJILLO

I n the Caribbean garlic is widely used in cooking—and religion! This sauce, popular on the Spanish-speaking islands, combines garlic with two other unique flavors: olives and capers. Serve it at room temperature over grilled chicken, fish, or steaks. Refrigerated, it will keep for three to four days.

1 bulb (whole head) garlic, separated into cloves	2½ cups olive oil
½ cup pitted green olives	2 egg yolks
	Salt to taste
½ cup drained capers	Freshly ground black pepper to taste

In a food processor, first chop the head of garlic. Add the olives, capers, and oil and process for about 2 minutes or until smooth in consistency. Add the egg yolks and process again to emulsify. Add salt and pepper to taste.

Yield: 2 pints

AJILIMOJILI

T his Latin-style pepper and garlic sauce combines hot and sweet peppers with garlic, coriander, lime, and vinegar. Its piquant flavor seems to go well with everything—meat, fish, and poultry, as well as salads and vegetables.

2 red peppers, seeded and quartered	2 sprigs fresh coriander, chopped
1 green pepper, seeded and quartered	Juice of 1 lime
	¼ cup malt vinegar
3 Scotch bonnet peppers, seeded	1 teaspoon salt
1 bulb (whole head) garlic, separated into cloves	1 tablespoon freshly ground black pepper
	½ cup olive oil

Puree the red peppers, green pepper, Scotch bonnet peppers, garlic, coriander, and lime juice in a food processor. Add the vinegar, salt, black pepper, and olive oil and process again. Bottle the sauce in hot sterilized jars.

Yield: 3 cups

Sauces

SAUCE CREOLE

This French West Indian sauce is especially good with grilled fish, chicken, or beef. Light and delicate in flavor, it will enhance almost any dish.

¾ cup olive oil	2 8-ounce cans tomato sauce
3 green peppers, finely chopped	1 cup white wine
1 white onion, finely chopped	1 tablespoon freshly ground black pepper
3 cloves garlic, minced	1 teaspoon salt
2 large tomatoes, diced	
1 Scotch bonnet pepper, seeded and finely chopped	

In a large skillet, heat the oil and sauté the green peppers, onion, and garlic until they are tender. Add the tomatoes and sauté for 5 to 10 minutes. Add the Scotch bonnet pepper, tomato sauce, wine, black pepper, and salt and stir well. Bring the mixture to a boil, lower the heat, and simmer, covered, for 15 to 20 minutes.

Yield: 4 pints

SAUCE CHIEN

Can you believe it? This is a recipe for "Dog Sauce," but don't let the name fool you. In the French West Indies, home of Sauce Chien, it is believed that this special potion is so incredible that it even makes dog taste good. But it is used on fish, poultry, and beef, we're glad to report, and also makes a dipping sauce for crispy French bread.

1 white onion, finely chopped	1 teaspoon salt
3 green onions, finely chopped	1 teaspoon freshly ground black pepper
3 cloves garlic, minced	1 cup boiling water
1 Scotch bonnet pepper, seeded and finely chopped	¼ cup olive oil
	¾ cup cider vinegar
3 sprigs fresh basil, finely chopped	1 tablespoon Dijon mustard
3 sprigs fresh parsley, finely chopped	Juice of 1 lime
	2 hard-cooked egg yolks, mashed

Place the onion, green onions, garlic, Scotch bonnet pepper, basil, parsley, salt, and black pepper in a heatproof bowl and pour the boiling water over them. Let stand so that the flavors blend. In a separate bowl, whisk together the oil, vinegar, mustard, and lime juice to make a vinaigrette. Add the chopped egg yolks, then stir into the onion-pepper mixture and combine well. Let the sauce stand, uncovered, at room temperature for at least 1 hour before serving.

Yield: 3½ cups

SALSA MOTAZA

his sassy mustard sauce, created by Pablo, is usually served on top of freshly grilled fish or fried breaded pork chops.

¼ cup Dijon mustard	1 teaspoon freshly ground black pepper
½ red onion, quartered	
½ stalk fresh coriander	1 egg
1 teaspoon salt	1 teaspoon lime juice
	½ cup olive oil

Place the mustard, onion, coriander, salt, pepper, egg, and lime juice in a blender or food processor and process for 1 minute. With the machine running, add the olive oil in a slow and steady stream. Process until the sauce thickens to the consistency of mayonnaise.

Yield: About 1 cup

SALSA NARANJA

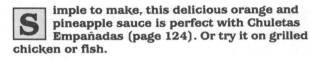imple to make, this delicious orange and pineapple sauce is perfect with Chuletas Empañadas (page 124). Or try it on grilled chicken or fish.

½ cup sugar	1 cup orange juice
1 cup water	2 tablespoons dark rum
2 oranges, sliced (with rind) and seeded	2 teaspoons cornstarch stirred into 2 tablespoons water
1 cup chopped fresh pineapple (about ½ pineapple)	

In a heavy saucepan, combine the sugar and water and simmer over low heat, stirring occasionally, until it starts to get syrupy. Add the oranges, pineapple, orange juice, and dark rum and simmer on low for about 20 minutes or until the orange rinds are soft. Remove the saucepan from the stove and strain the sauce. Discard the orange rinds and place the sauce back in the saucepan. Mix in the cornstarch and simmer again until the sauce thickens, stirring well.

Yield: About 5 cups

MANGO CHUTNEY

Chutneys were introduced by East Indian workers who were brought to the islands, and today they are an integral part of Caribbean cuisine. Most often they are served with curry dishes or used as glazes for meats and poultry.

8 cups peeled and diced green mangoes	4 cups brown sugar
1 pound dark raisins	2 tablespoons mustard seed
1 pound pitted dates, chopped	2 Scotch bonnet peppers, seeded and finely chopped
1 cup finely chopped fresh ginger	1 pound white onions, finely chopped
1 bulb (whole head) garlic, finely chopped	2 tablespoons salt
	8 cups malt vinegar

In a Dutch oven, combine all the ingredients and bring to a boil over moderate heat, stirring occasionally. Lower the heat and simmer the mixture, uncovered, for 45 minutes or until the chutney is thick and brown. Let the chutney cool completely before serving. Bottle, if you like, in hot sterilized jars. It gets better with age.

Yield: 4 pints

MANGO CHUTNEY GLAZE

This aromatic glaze was created by our chef using garlic, onion, and hot sauce to contrast with the sweetness of the mango. Try brushing it on fish, chicken, or pork chops and then baking them for a simple but delectable meal. The glaze can be stored in the refrigerator almost indefinitely.

¼ cup (½ stick) butter	1 12-ounce jar mango chutney (or 1½ cups Mango Chutney, left)
2 cloves garlic, minced	
1 small white onion, finely chopped	2 tablespoons (1 ounce) Cointreau
	Dash hot red pepper sauce

In a heavy saucepan, melt the butter over moderate heat and sauté the garlic and onion until they are limp. Mix in the chutney and Cointreau and stir until the sauce begins to bubble. Lower the heat and simmer until the mixture begins to thicken, about 15 minutes, stirring occasionally. Remove from the heat, add the dash of hot pepper sauce, and stir.

Yield: 2 cups

MANGO PEPPERPOT

Almost every island boasts several varieties of fruit relishes. They are great with any meal, day or night. This one is sweet and spicy hot and tastes great with grilled chicken.

3	mangoes, peeled, seeded, and thinly sliced
1	large white onion, finely chopped
2	Scotch bonnet peppers, seeded and finely chopped
¼	cup white vinegar
¼	cup olive oil
½	tablespoon salt
½	tablespoon freshly ground black pepper

In a large bowl, combine all the ingredients and mix well. Cover and refrigerate for at least 1 hour before serving. The longer you wait, the better.

Yield: 2½ pints

PICKLED ONIONS

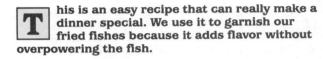

This is an easy recipe that can really make a dinner special. We use it to garnish our fried fishes because it adds flavor without overpowering the fish.

1½	quarts water
1½	quarts white vinegar
3	Spanish onions, thinly sliced
3	allspice berries
3	peppercorns
1	Scotch bonnet pepper, seeded and finely chopped

Place all the ingredients in a large saucepan, and bring to a boil over high heat. Boil for 10 minutes and remove from the stove. Let the pan stand at room temperature for 15 to 20 minutes. Drain the onions and serve immediately on top of grilled meats or fish. The onions will keep in the refrigerator for 1 week.

Yield: 3 cups

Sauces

RED PEPPER REMOULADE

C reole in character, this traditional sauce can be used in salads or with seafood, chicken, or beef. Very versatile, it tastes good on just about everything.

1 red pepper, seeded and roughly chopped	3 tablespoons chopped fresh parsley
1 tablespoon sweet paprika	1 clove garlic
1 teaspoon salt	3 tablespoons tomato sauce
1 teaspoon freshly ground black pepper	2 egg yolks
	1 cup Dijon mustard

Place the red pepper, paprika, salt, black pepper, parsley, garlic, tomato sauce, and egg yolks in a blender or food processor and process for 1 minute. Add the mustard and process another 2 minutes or until the pepper and garlic are pureed and the sauce is thick.

Yield: About 2 cups

BUBBA'S TOMATO BUTTER

B ubba Lou's Crab Cakes (page 77) are just plain good without this sauce, but with it they are sensational. Try it also as a dipping sauce for boiled shrimp or fried clams.

1 tablespoon chopped tomato skins	5 green onions, finely chopped
¾ cup ketchup	5 cloves garlic, minced
1 teaspoon dried thyme	1 cup (2 sticks) unsalted butter, chilled
1 teaspoon dried marjoram	

In a heavy skillet, combine the tomato skins, ketchup, thyme, marjoram, green onions, and garlic. Simmer over moderate heat for about 5 minutes, stirring constantly. Lower the heat and slowly add the butter, stirring to prevent browning. When the butter has completely melted and combined with the other ingredients, remove it from the stove and serve it with crab cakes.

Yield: 2½ cups

PINEAPPLE VINAIGRETTE

 Pineapples grow best in the climate of the Caribbean, especially on the volcanic islands, where the soil has high acid levels. It is a versatile fruit and plays a major role in island cuisine. This sweet and tangy vinaigrette is excellent on seafood salads as well as fruit salad.

¾	cup olive oil	2	cloves garlic, minced
	Juice of 1 lime		
⅓	cup white vinegar	2	tablespoons Dijon mustard
¼	cup fresh pineapple juice	1	teaspoon salt
		1	teaspoon freshly ground black pepper

In a bowl, mix all the ingredients together with a wire whisk until the oil and liquids are well combined. Serve at room temperature.

Yield: 2 cups

FRESH LIME SAUCE

Fruit salad tastes wonderful topped with this simple sauce. It can be stored, refrigerated, for three to four days.

1	cup plain yogurt	¼	teaspoon ground nutmeg
⅓	cup sugar	¼	teaspoon ground ginger
	Juice of 3 limes		

In a bowl, mix all the ingredients together with a wire whisk until smooth and creamy. Cover and refrigerate at least 30 minutes before serving.

Yield: 2 cups

SAUCE AVOCAT

Another versatile sauce, this avocado puree can be made mild or hot, depending on the amount of hot sauce you put in. It can be used with fish, meats, chicken, and vegetables and will keep well in the refrigerator for three to four days.

5 to 6 ripe avocados, peeled, pitted, and cubed

2 cups lime juice

1 large white onion, roughly chopped

6 sprigs fresh coriander leaves

3 sprigs fresh parsley leaves

1 clove garlic

1 tablespoon freshly ground black pepper

1 tablespoon white pepper

2 tablespoons salt

¼ cup chopped pimiento-stuffed green olives

2 tablespoons drained capers

½ cup white wine

¼ cup passion fruit juice or orange juice

Dash hot red pepper sauce

Place the avocados, lime juice, onion, coriander, parsley, garlic, black pepper, white pepper, salt, olives, and capers in a food processor and puree until creamy. Add the wine, fruit juice, and hot pepper sauce and process again. Serve at room temperature.

Yield: 5 pints

AVOCADO MAYONNAISE

Fish, lobster, salads, meats—just about everything is enhanced by this lovely green dressing, which is common on the French-speaking islands. It is great because it can be made in advance and stored in the refrigerator for three to four days.

2 ripe avocados, pitted, peeled, and mashed

1 cup mayonnaise

1 Scotch bonnet pepper, seeded and finely chopped

4 cloves garlic, minced

1 small white onion, finely chopped

2 teaspoons salt

2 teaspoons freshly ground black pepper

Juice of 4 limes

Place all the ingredients in a food processor or blender and puree until smooth and creamy. Chill or serve at room temperature.

Yield: 2½ pints

Beverages

PLANTER'S PUNCH

How many ways are there to make Planter's Punch? How many bartenders are there in Jamaica? Everyone has a favorite recipe, but basically this drink is a mixture of dark rum with fruit juices. The following is a fairly typical concoction that we serve at Sugar Reef.

Juice of 1 orange	2 ounces dark rum
Juice of 1 lime	3 teaspoons confectioner's sugar
Juice of 1 lemon	
3 dashes grenadine	Orange slice, for garnish
½ cup pineapple juice	

In a mixing glass, combine the citrus juices, grenadine, pineapple juice, rum, and sugar. Stir gently and pour into a tall glass over cracked ice. Garnish with an orange slice.

Serves 1

PATIO PUNCH

This easy punch is a sure crowd pleaser. It simplifies party-giving because it can be prepared well in advance.

1 750-ml bottle dark rum	1 2-liter bottle ginger ale
2 cups grapefruit juice	Lime slices, for garnish
1 cup lime juice	

Combine the rum, grapefruit juice, and lime juice and chill in the refrigerator. When you are ready to serve, pour over ice in a large punch bowl and add the ginger ale. Garnish with slices of lime.

Yield: 3½ quarts

Beverages

BAJAN RUM PUNCH

Folks on Barbados are very serious about their rum punches. Two distinctive ingredients—nutmeg and bitters—are integral to this cocktail and must not be omitted if you want a true Bajan-style punch. This recipe came to us from our friend Daphne, who manages the Buccaneer Bay Hotel in St. James.

1 ounce dark Bajan rum	1 ounce lime juice
½ ounce Falernum (page 215) or simple syrup	Splash of bitters
	Pinch of ground nutmeg, for garnish
	Lime wedge, for garnish

In a mixing glass, combine the rum, simple syrup, and lime juice and shake well. Pour into a rocks glass filled with ice and splash with bitters. Sprinkle nutmeg on top and garnish with a lime wedge.

Serves 1

Bajan-Style Punch

Another Bajan rum punch follows a formula that is simple and fun to remember: "One of sour, two of sweet, three of strong, and four of weak." That is,

1 part lime juice
2 parts sugar
3 parts rum
4 parts juice or water

TI PUNCH

The name *Ti* is a contracted version of *Petite*. This rum punch is best when prepared with a white rum from Martinique or Guadeloupe, which produce the best white rums we have sampled. If you are not able to locate sugar cane syrup, try Falernum (page 215) as a substitute.

2 ounces white rum	½ ounce lime juice
1 ounce sugar cane syrup	Lime wedge, for garnish

In a mixing glass, combine the rum, syrup, and lime juice and shake well. Pour into a tall glass filled with ice and garnish with a lime wedge.

Serves 1

RUM BOOGIE

This recipe is a jazzed-up version of the Cuba Libre. Amaretto is the ingredient that gives this classic a new twist. Serve it with plenty of fresh lime.

3	lime wedges	½	ounce Amaretto liqueur
1½	ounces dark rum	2	ounces cola

Over a highball glass, squeeze the lime wedges well. This causes the oil in the rind to come out. Fill the glass with ice and add the rum, Amaretto, and cola. Stir well and serve.

Serves 1

DARK AND STORMY

Popular on many islands, especially Barbados, this drink combines the zing of real ginger beer with the smoothness of a rich dark rum. Its name comes from the bold yet smooth taste.

1½	ounces dark rum	Lime wedge, for garnish
3	ounces Ginger Beer (page 214)	

In a mixing glass, combine the rum and ginger beer and shake well. Pour into a rocks glass filled with ice and garnish with a plastic seahorse and a wedge of lime.

Serves 1

Beverages

STUYVESANT COOLER

A s you can tell by the name, this refreshing drink originated in the Netherland Antilles, where Peter Stuyvesant was governor before he went to New York. The primary flavoring comes from Curaçao, a liqueur made from the peel of the famous green oranges grown on that island.

1½ ounces light rum	½ ounce lime juice
½ ounce Curaçao	Orange slice, for garnish
½ ounce simple syrup	

In a mixing glass, combine the rum, Curaçao, simple syrup, and lime juice. Shake well and pour over ice in a tall glass. Garnish with an orange slice.

Serves 1

MAI-TAI

T he Mai-Tai is a popular tropical cocktail, often requested by our customers. It did not originate in the West Indies but in the South Pacific. However, we felt the Mai Tai qualified for inclusion in this book because it contains ingredients that are found in the Caribbean. The addition of a fine Caribbean dark rum makes it perfect.

2 ounces dark rum	½ ounce orgeat syrup (almond flavor)
½ ounce Triple Sec	
1 ounce lemon juice	Fresh mint sprig, for garnish
1 ounce simple syrup	Orange slice, for garnish
½ ounce Roses lime juice	

In a mixing glass, combine the rum, Triple Sec, lemon juice, simple syrup, Roses lime juice, and orgeat syrup and shake well. Pour into a tall frosted glass filled with ice. Garnish with fresh mint and a slice of orange.

Serves 1

Simple Sugar

Bartenders prefer to use simple sugar, also called sugar syrup, because even superfine sugar doesn't dissolve well in cold drinks. It is simply a mixture of equal parts water and sugar and measures the same: 1 teaspoon simple sugar equals 1 teaspoon sugar.

UNCLE ALBERT'S SMASH

G rapefruit is a native fruit of the Caribbean, and its juice is most delicious when freshly squeezed. When shopping for grapefruit, buy large, firm ones with fine-grained skins. Uncle Albert is ninety years old and credits this concoction (and dating young women) for his long, healthy life.

1 ounce white rum	2 ounces grapefruit juice
1 ounce gin	Fresh mint sprig, for garnish
½ ounce orgeat syrup (almond flavor)	

In a mixing glass, combine the rum, gin, orgeat syrup, and grapefruit juice. Shake well and pour over ice in a rocks glass. Garnish with a fresh mint sprig.

Serves 1

ZOMBIE!

W arning—more than one of these is likely to turn you into one. For a tamer version, omit the 151 rum, which packs quite a wallop.

1 ounce white rum	½ ounce Roses lime juice
1½ ounces dark rum	1 ounce pineapple juice
½ ounce 151-proof rum	1 ounce papaya nectar
	Fresh pineapple wedge, for garnish

In a mixing glass, combine the white rum, dark rum, 151 rum, Roses lime juice, pineapple juice, and papaya juice and shake well. Pour into a tall glass filled with ice. Garnish with a pineapple wedge and a plastic palm tree.

Serves 1

Beverages

YELLOW BIRD

Yellow bird, "sittin' high in banana tree," is a classic Caribbean tune. The Yellow Bird cocktail, however, gets its name from its glorious color. It combines the yellow and orange of two fruit juices with the golden color of rum.

1½ ounces gold rum	¼ ounce orgeat syrup (almond flavor)
1 ounce orange juice	
1 ounce pineapple juice	Orange slice, for garnish

In a mixing glass, combine the rum, orange juice, pineapple juice, and orgeat syrup and shake well. Pour into a tall glass filled with ice and garnish with an orange slice.

Serves 1

Yellow Bird
Traditional

Yellow bird, up high in banana tree,
Yellow bird, sits all alone like me.
Did your lady friend
Leave the nest again?
That is very bad,
Makes you feel so sad.
She can fly away
In the sky all day,
Share more laughter than me.
Yellow bird, up high in banana tree,
Better fly away
In the sky away
Pick is coming soon
Picks from nine to noon.
Let them yell at you
Like banana do,
They may pick you someday.

CHIPPIE'S BAHAMA MAMA

This drink came to Sugar Reef through a good friend, Chip, a frequent traveler to the Bahamas who has great connections with the local bartenders. There are many other ways to prepare this drink, but none of them top this version.

1½ ounces dark rum	Splash of grenadine
1½ ounces rum liqueur	Orange slice, for garnish
1 ounce orange juice	Maraschino cherry, for garnish
1 ounce pineapple juice	

In a mixing glass, combine the rum, rum liqueur, orange juice, pineapple juice, and grenadine. Shake well and pour over ice in a tall frosted glass. Garnish with an orange slice and maraschino cherry.

Serves 1

GOOMBAY SMASH

We learned about this wild and delicious cocktail while attending the Goombay Festival in the Bahamas. We goombayed the night away and felt the smash the next morning.

1 ounce dark rum

1 ounce light rum

2 ounces pineapple juice

½ ounce Coco Lopez (sweetened cream of coconut)

In a mixing glass, combine the dark rum, light rum, pineapple juice, and Coco Lopez and shake well. Pour into a tall glass filled with ice and garnish with a hanging beach ball.

Serves 1

DOWN COMFORTER

If anything can beat the cold winter in New York, this drink certainly can. Combine some warm ingredients from the islands and lightly shake.

1 ounce white rum

½ ounce Southern Comfort

1 ounce Coco Lopez (sweetened cream of coconut)

1 ounce heavy cream

Shredded coconut

In a mixing glass, combine the rum, Southern Comfort, Coco Lopez, and heavy cream and shake well. Pour into a rocks glass filled with ice and sprinkle the top with coconut.

Serves 1

Beverages

LATIN MANHATTAN

When Sugar Reef was about to open, our good friend Russell decided it would be great fun to create a Caribbean-style drink for the bar. He came up with the Latin Manhattan, which fits the restaurant perfectly. It follows the tradition of the Manhattan cocktail but with a Caribbean twist.

2½ ounces Captain Morgan's Spiced Rum

Splash of sweet vermouth

Maraschino cherry, for garnish

Combine the rum and vermouth in a rocks glass filled with ice. Garnish with a cherry and a miniature plastic mermaid.

Serves 1

SAN JUAN BLOODY MARY

Puerto Rico is regarded as the leading producer of white or light-bodied rums. In fact, the world's largest rum distillery is The Bacardi plant in San Juan. Try making this Latin variation on the classic vodka drink using different types of rum, including dark.

1½ ounces light rum

4 ounces V-8 cocktail juice

2 tablespoons lime juice

4 dashes Worcestershire sauce

4 dashes Tabasco sauce

Salt to taste

Black pepper to taste

Coriander sprig, for garnish

Combine all the ingredients in a shaker glass and mix well. Pour over ice in a tall glass and garnish with a sprig of coriander.

Serves 1

MARGARITA

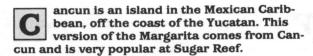**C**ancun is an island in the Mexican Caribbean, off the coast of the Yucatan. This version of the Margarita comes from Cancun and is very popular at Sugar Reef.

2 ounces tequila	1 ounce Roses lime juice
1 ounce Cointreau	Salt (optional)
½ ounce lemon juice	Lime wedge, for garnish

ON THE ROCKS:
In a mixing glass, combine the tequila, Cointreau, lemon juice, and Roses lime juice and shake well. For a Margarita with salt, wet the rim of a rocks glass with lemon juice and invert on a saucer of salt. Fill the glass with ice and pour the Margarita on top. Garnish with a wedge of lime.

FROZEN:
In a blender, combine the tequila, Cointreau, lemon juice, Roses lime juice, and a scoop of crushed ice. Blend until smooth and pour into a tall glass or large martini glass (see above for a Margarita with salt). Garnish with a wedge of lime.

Serves 1

CHAMPAGNE CARIBE

**C**hampagne drinkers, here is the cocktail for you. It adds the fruity flavors of orange and banana without overpowering the sparkle and crispness of the champagne. One or two of these will have you daydreaming of the islands.

½ ounce white rum	Splash of orange bitters
Splash of vodka	Champagne
Splash of banana liqueur	Banana slice, for garnish

Combine the rum, vodka, banana liqueur, and bitters in a champagne glass and fill with champagne. Garnish with a banana slice and a fresh flower.

Serves 1

Beverages

TROPICAL MIMOSA

Here is another way to present the traditional mimosa. The flavor of the mango or papaya with champagne is different and very refreshing. Use fresh nectar if at all possible.

2 ounces mango or papaya nectar	Champagne

Combine the nectar and champagne and lightly stir. Serve in a champagne glass.

Serves 1

CORAL REEF

This frozen drink gets its name from its beautiful coral color. It was created at Sugar Reef and is garnished with a large plastic gardenia.

1½ ounces dark rum	½ ounce grenadine
1 ounce lemon juice	1 scoop crushed ice
1 ounce simple syrup	

Combine the rum, lemon juice, simple syrup, grenadine, and crushed ice in a blender until smooth. Serve in a large martini glass and garnish with a flower.

Serves 1

Frozen Drinks

The widespread popularity of frozen drinks that has developed over the past few years has given a new twist to old favorites like the daiquiri, Margarita, and piña colada. These summer refreshers can be made in any blender with a few cubes of ice. The recipes on these pages call for a scoop (like an ice cream scoop) of crushed ice, but if you don't have an ice machine, just substitute three to four ice cubes. For quicker results and less noise, wrap the cubes in a dish towel and smash them a few times with a mallet before adding to the blender.

ALIZÉ DAIQUIRI

A lizé is a liqueur from France that combines passion fruit with cognac. We got the idea to combine it with our daiquiri recipe and it became an instant hit.

1 ounce Alizé liqueur	½ ounce simple syrup
2 ounces white rum	1 scoop crushed ice
½ ounce Triple Sec	Fresh mint sprig, for garnish
1 ounce lime juice	Lime wedge, for garnish

Combine the Alizé, rum, Triple Sec, lime juice, simple syrup, and ice in a blender until smooth. Pour into a tall glass and garnish with a sprig of fresh mint and a lime wedge.

Serves 1

FRUIT DAIQUIRI

T his well-known drink had its greatest popularity during the late 1950s and early '60s when Havana was still a chic resort. It is having a renaissance due to the renewed popularity of rums from throughout the islands. Lime is the traditional base, but other fruits make sensational variations.

2 ounces white rum	4 strawberries or ½ banana or juice of ½ lime or 1 ounce Coco Lopez (sweetened cream of coconut)
½ ounce Triple Sec	
1 ounce lemon juice	
½ ounce simple syrup	1 scoop crushed ice
	Lime wedge, for garnish

Combine the rum, Triple Sec, lemon juice, simple syrup, fruit, and ice in a blender until smooth and creamy. Serve in a tall glass, garnished with a lime wedge and paper fan.

Serves 1

Beverages

RHUMBA PUNCH

Smooth and fruity, this frozen drink is a big favorite at Sugar Reef. Our creative bar manager whipped it up and our customers demanded it be kept on the menu permanently.

1 ounce dark rum	4 strawberries, tops removed
½ ounce Midori liqueur	1 scoop crushed ice
2 ounces orange juice	Orange slice, for garnish

Combine the rum, Midori, orange juice, strawberries, and crushed ice in a blender until smooth. Pour into a tall glass and garnish with an orange slice and a paper fan.

Serves 1

THE HUMMINGBIRD

Thank the Japanese for Midori, a recent addition to our shelf of fruit-flavored liqueurs. This lovely green one is made from honeydew melons and mixes perfectly with typical island ingredients to give us new variations in tropical libations.

½ ounce Midori liqueur	1 scoop crushed ice
1½ ounces white rum	Splash of grenadine
1½ ounces mango nectar	

Combine the Midori, rum, mango nectar, and ice in a blender until smooth. Top with a splash of grenadine and blend one more time. Pour into a tall glass and serve.

Serves 1

Rum

There are many types of rums throughout the Caribbean, and they vary from island to island. There are very dry, light-bodied rums found on the Spanish-speaking islands; rich, full-bodied rums on the English-speaking islands; and light, aromatic rums on the French-speaking islands. Rum is a by-product of sugar cane and is distilled from molasses. It is aged in oak barrels, usually one to three years, sometimes six depending upon the blend desired. Rum is an integral part of island life and is drunk every day. It is used to toast the arrival of a new baby, welcome a child's christening, celebrate a marriage, or even mourn a death.

SURF SIDER

This is by far the most popular tropical libation at Sugar Reef. It was inspired by a trip to the Bahamas, where we sipped several while overlooking the ocean. We serve this fun cocktail in a ceramic glass that depicts a young island girl on a surfboard. It is garnished with a tissue beach ball.

2 ounces white rum	½ ounce simple syrup
1 ounce blue Curaçao	1 scoop crushed ice
2 ounces pineapple juice	

Combine the rum, blue Curaçao, pineapple juice, simple syrup, and ice in a blender until smooth. Serve in the wackiest glass you can find.

Serves 1

PIÑA COLADA

Many people who do not know a great deal about the Caribbean do know about the Piña Colada. The creator of this concoction was a genius or just plain lucky! Pineapple and coconut are natural partners and, when teamed with dark rum, make an unbeatable combination.

1½ ounces dark rum	1 scoop crushed ice
2 ounces pineapple juice	Pineapple slice, for garnish
½ ounce Coco Lopez (sweetened cream of coconut)	

Combine the rum, pineapple juice, Coco Lopez, and ice in a blender until smooth. Serve in a tall glass and garnish with a fresh pineapple slice.

Serves 1

Beverages

MANDARINE COLADA

This recipe is a variation on the classic Piña Colada. It combines the colada character with the zesty citrus flavor of orange. Who would have thought you could improve on the original!

1½ ounces dark rum	½ ounce Coco Lopez (sweetened cream of coconut)
1 ounce Mandarine Napolean	
2 ounces pineapple juice	1 scoop crushed ice
	Fresh orange slice, for garnish

Combine the rum, Mandarine Napolean, pineapple juice, Coco Lopez, and ice in a blender until smooth. Serve in a tall glass and garnish with an orange slice.

Serves 1

COCO BATITA

Actually a Brazilian cocktail, this after-dinner drink came to Sugar Reef through our waitress Patricia, a native of Brazil. It blends the rich flavor of coconut and fresh cream with a liqueur made from sugar cane.

1½ ounces dark Brazilian sugar cane liqueur	1 ounce Coco Lopez (sweetened cream of coconut)
1 ounce heavy cream	Shredded coconut

In a mixing glass, combine the liqueur, cream, and Coco Lopez and shake well. Pour into a rocks glass filled with ice. Garnish the top with shredded coconut.

Serves 1

COCO CAFE

his is dessert and coffee all in one. Coco Ribe, which is available at most liquor store, blends coconut with rum liqueur.

½   cup freshly brewed coffee

1½ ounces Coco Ribe liqueur

1¼ ounces dark rum

Whipped cream

Shredded coconut, for garnish

Fill a coffee mug halfway with hot coffee. Stir in the Coco Ribe and dark rum and top with whipped cream. Sprinkle coconut on top and serve.

Serves 1

FLAMINGO DIABLO

his drink is most popular in the dead of New York winters. It's not just a hot brew—it's actually on fire. Use caution in preparing this concoction. We serve it in a fancy skull mug.

1   ounce white rum

½   ounce Coco Lopez (sweetened cream of coconut)

½   cup freshly brewed coffee

1   ounce 151-proof rum

Combine the white rum, Coco Lopez, and coffee in a mug. Add the 151 rum and ignite. Serve immediately, but be sure the flame is blown out before sipping.

Serves 1

Beverages

JAMAICAN JAVA

 Rich and delicious, this after-dinner coffee should be made only with good Caribbean rum. It makes all the difference in the world.

1 **ounce white rum**	**Whipped cream**
1½ **ounces Jamaican Crème Liqueur**	**Ground nutmeg, for garnish**
½ **cup freshly brewed coffee**	

In a coffee cup, combine the rum, Jamaican Crème Liqueur, and coffee. Spoon whipped cream on top and sprinkle with nutmeg. Serve immediately.

Serves 1

PARADISE PUNCH

At one time there was a large selection of rum drinks on our menu but not many nonalcoholic drinks to choose from. So we created this and our customers love it.

2 **teaspoons chopped fresh ginger**	2½ **cups pineapple juice**
7 **cups water**	2½ **cups orange juice**
1¾ **cups sugar**	½ **cup lemon juice**
1½ **cups guava nectar**	**Fresh mint sprigs, for garnish**

Boil the ginger in 3 cups of the water for about 30 minutes. Cool and strain through a cloth, squeezing well to extract most of the ginger flavor. Boil the sugar in the remaining water until it begins to thicken and becomes syrupy. Cool. In a large pitcher, combine all the ingredients and chill. Serve in tall glasses over ice and garnish with fresh mint sprigs.

Serves 12

TROPICAL ICE

 his is a quick and easy summertime pick-me-up that kids love.

4 ripe bananas, peeled

½ cup sugar

Juice of 4 oranges

Juice of 4 limes

½ cup water

In a large bowl, mash the bananas well and combine with the sugar. Stir in the orange and lime juices and water and stir until thoroughly mixed. Pour into ice trays or individual serving cups and freeze for about 4 hours.

Serves 4

GINGER BEER

 he best ginger in the world is said to be grown in the West Indies, and its most popular use is in ginger beer. This beverage is nonalcoholic, yet a strong stimulant (helpful if you have a bad cold). It is also a great cocktail when mixed with dark rum.

¾ cup grated fresh ginger

6 cups boiling water

Juice of 2 limes

1½ cups sugar

½ teaspoon dried yeast

Combine all the ingredients, stir well, and place in a large container. Seal tightly and leave at room temperature for at least 24 hours. Strain and refrigerate until completely chilled.

Yield: 2 quarts

Beverages

FRESH FRUIT BATITAS

Batitas are extremely popular on many of the Spanish islands, where they are readily available from roadside vendors and cafes. Just about any fruit in season can be used. You can mix the fruits or even add a bit of rum for more punch.

BANANA BATITA
½ peeled banana
1½ ounces banana nectar
½ ounce milk
1 scoop crushed ice

MANGO BATITA
2 slices fresh mango
1½ ounces mango nectar
½ ounce milk
1 scoop crushed ice

PAPAYA BATITA
2 slices fresh papaya
1½ ounces papaya nectar
½ ounce milk
1 scoop crushed ice

PINEAPPLE BATITA
2 slices fresh pineapple
1½ ounces pineapple juice
½ ounce milk
1 scoop crushed ice

Place all the ingredients for a batita in a blender and puree until smooth and creamy.

Serves 1

FALERNUM

Falernum is a spiced sugar syrup used to flavor rum punches and other rum cocktails. A prosperous Barbadian plantation owner created it from sugar cane. The liqueur's main ingredients are lime and sugar. It has an extremely pleasant taste and can be very potent.

2 quarts water
2 pounds sugar
¾ cup lime juice, strained

2 tablespoons almond extract
1 tablespoon ground nutmeg
¼ cup dark rum

In a large saucepan, bring the water to a brisk boil. Pour in the sugar and stir until it begins to dissolve. Lower the heat and simmer for 5 to 10 minutes, stirring occasionally. Add the lime juice, almond extract, nutmeg, and rum and stir to combine all the ingredients. Simmer for another 10 to 15 minutes. Remove the saucepan from the stove and let the liquid cool to room temperature. Pour the Falernum into empty rum bottles and use as flavoring in Bajan Rum Punch (page 199).

Yield: About 4 quarts

GLOSSARY

Accra. A fritter usually made with flaked codfish.

Ajillo. A Spanish garlic sauce made with chopped capers and olives.

Annatto oil. Oil that has been soaked with annatto seed to give it a bright red color that adds to the attractiveness of foods cooked in it.

Annatto seed. The small red seed of the annatto tree, used to color foods. Paprika is an excellent substitute.

Aubergine. The French word for eggplant; also a term used by the British.

Avocado. A pear-shaped vegetable with a thick, alligatorlike skin that encloses a creamy, green, flavorful pulp. It is used in salads and soups.

Bacalaito. The Spanish word for codfish fritter.

Bacalao. The Spanish term for dried salt cod.

Banana leaf. Used to wrap fish, meat, or spiced yam or cassava for steam cooking. It imparts a light, delicate flavor to foods.

Batita. A Spanish fruit drink made with ice, fresh fruit, and milk. May be nonalcoholic or spiked with rum.

Blaff. A technique of poaching fish in delicately seasoned water.

Bouquet garni. Aromatic herbs tied together with string if fresh or in cheesecloth if dried, then added to soups and stews for flavor. It often includes parsley, celery, green onion, thyme, and bay leaf.

Calabaza. A West Indian pumpkin that tastes similar to the American pumpkin but is a bit sweeter. Its outer skin is much like that of an acorn squash. It is known as *giraumon* on the French islands.

Calaloo. A leafy vegetable very similar to spinach in flavor and appearance. It is the main ingredient in a hearty stew or soup that bears its name and is seasoned with crab, pork, or okra. Kale or spinach is an acceptable substitute.

Camarón. The Spanish word for shrimp.

Caper. Usually packed in vinegar, this is the flower bud of the caper bush. Full of flavor, capers are frequently used in the seasoning of Spanish dishes.

Cassava. Also known as yucca or manioc, this root vegetable comes in two varieties, sweet and bitter. The white pulp is usually boiled and prepared as a vegetable. The bitter cassava is considered poisonous before it is cooked.

Cayenne. A powdered spice made from dried hot peppers. It is very potent.

Chayote. The Spanish word for a pear-shaped vegetable with a ridged skin; called *christophene* on the French islands. It tastes similar to summer squash and is usually boiled and stuffed with seafood fillings.

Christophene. *See* Chayote.

Chuleta. The Spanish word for pork chop.

Chutney. A condiment brought to the West Indies from the East Indies. Often made of chopped green mangoes, raisins, onions, and spices, it is customarily served with curries.

Coconut cream. *See page 10.*

Coriander. Known as *cilantro* in Spanish, this long, leafy herb is used extensively throughout the Caribbean to flavor foods. It has a distinctive taste and is most popular on the Spanish islands.

Conch. *See page 11.*

Cilantro. *See* Coriander.

Curaçao. An orange liqueur made from the bitter green oranges grown on the island of Curaçao. It has a distinctive blue color.

Eddo. A tuber vegetable that is very similar to the ordinary potato and is common in the West Indies.

Falernum. A sugar cane syrup spiced with nutmeg and lime (page 215), created on Barbados. It is used in rum punches and for glazing meats.

Flan. A baked custard that has a caramelized sugar topping. It is popular on all the islands.

Ginger. A root that, when peeled and grated, has a hot yet sweet flavor. It made its way to the Caribbean via Chinese slaves and is widely used to make chutneys, ginger beer, and ginger ale.

Groundnut. Another name for the peanut.

Gruyère. A flavorful hard cheese used for most of the au gratin dishes served on the French islands.

Guava. A sweet fruit used most often to make desserts, drinks, and jams.

Heart of palm. The tender center of the palm tree stalk that, when sliced, is excellent in salads and sauces. It is available canned in water.

Jalapeño. A small green chili pepper that is popular throughout Latin America. It is very hot.

Jamaican thyme. A variety of thyme that is grown in Jamaica and is stronger in flavor than its common counterpart. Available only in specialty stores.

Kale. A leafy green vegetable that is a good substitute for calaloo or spinach.

Kidney beans. Also known as the red bean or *habichuela* in Spanish.

Langosta. The Spanish word for lobster. Those native to the Caribbean do not have a big claw.

Langouste. The French word for lobster.

Mango. When ripe, this Caribbean fruit is sweet, juicy, and aromatic and is eaten raw or used in drinks, desserts, and jams. Unripe or green, it is used to make chutneys or in vegetable dishes.

Morue. The French word for codfish.

Okra. A long, fuzzy, fingerlike vegetable that grows on vines and was brought to the Caribbean by African slaves. It is used in calaloo and gumbo.

Papaya. This tropical fruit, popular in desserts, drinks, and salads, is considered a natural meat tenderizer as well.

Pigeon peas. Cooked with rice and coconut milk to create peas 'n' rice, a national favorite in Barbados. Also known as congo or gongo peas.

Pilau. A rice dish that combines vegetables and spices with seafood and chicken.

Plantain. A member of the banana family that can be eaten only when cooked. Much larger than its banana cousin, it is eaten as both a vegetable and a fruit. When green, it is either boiled or baked like a potato, and when ripe, it is sliced and fried and has a sweet taste.

Pollo. The Spanish word for chicken.

Poulet. The French word for chicken.

Salsa. The Spanish word for sauce.

Scotch bonnet pepper. One of the most widely used peppers on the islands in the Caribbean, this fiery hot pepper gets its name from its bonnet shape. It can be replaced with any other hot pepper such as the serrano or jalapeño.

Sopa. The Spanish word for soup.

Sweet potato. A tuber vegetable with a yellow or orange flesh that is widely used in baking and cooking. It should not be confused with the yam, which belongs to an entirely different botanical family.

West Indian pumpkin. *See* Calabaza.

Yam. This tuber is indigenous to the tropics and should not be confused with the Louisiana yam, which is actually a sweet potato. It has yellow to white flesh and a thick and hairy outer skin.

INDEX

ACKNOWLEDGMENTS

*T*his cookbook was a special joy for me. Having grown up on the Gulf Coast of Louisiana and Mississippi, I rediscovered my own Creole/French roots and was easily able to parallel the foods and customs of my youth with those of the islands. But a cookbook, especially one like this, is not an individual achievement. Many others contributed to the final result. Special thanks and appreciation go to Sugar Reef's chef, Pablo Rosado, and my beloved partner, Zeet Peabody. These gentlemen are the geniuses responsible for every incredible dish of food served at the restaurant. Their endless supply of fabulous recipes and their love and laughter supported me throughout this project. I couldn't have done it without them. I can never thank enough two people who kept it all in perspective for me; my partner Jay Savulich and my sister Dawn Dedeaux. Their assistance in researching the history of the Caribbean and its food was invaluable. We are indebted to Ken Gumbs of the Caribbean Cultural Center in New York and Gene Cowell, publisher of Island Property Reports, for providing us with information on the Caribbean.

Special acknowledgment is due a person who was a tremendous source of inspiration to all of us at Sugar Reef, Madame Prudence Marcelin of Guadeloupe. She graced our kitchen for seven glorious days that changed our lives. We are grateful to Myron Clement and Joe Petrocik for making her guest stint possible with the assistance of Eric Rotin of the Guadeloupe Office of Tourism and also for introducing us to another wonderful friend, Jacques Guannel, the Director of Tourism in Martinique. We thank you, Jacques, for rolling out the red carpet on our trip to your island and for the highlight of the trip, a twelve-course meal at the restaurant/home of Madame Clotilde Paladino, our next guest chef, that will never

be forgotten. Daphne Warner, our Caribbean adviser and ambassador of goodwill, made life easy for us on all our island getaways. Keep island hopping—wherever you go, we go.

A million thanks to Susan Meyer and Marsha Melnick of Roundtable Press, who believed in the book and guided me through the entire project. Their undying encouragement and patience saw me through, laughing all the way. We thank you also for your wisdom in choice of publisher and editor in McGraw-Hill and Joan Nagy. It has been a wonderful experience working with them both. This book would not have been possible without the clever and humorous Ginny Croft, who filled in many gaps and gave life to its pages. My heartfelt thanks and praise to her. I was so grateful to finally have the opportunity to work with a dear and gifted friend, Andrea Mistretta, who completely understood what Sugar Reef the restaurant and the people were all about and designed a cover that is better than we could ever have hoped for. I also wish to acknowledge the artistic skills of three very talented people—designer Joan Peckolick, border artist Richard Manigault, and map artist Wendy Frost—who captured the spunk and spirit of Sugar Reef so well throughout the book.

For all of their encouragement and taste-testing on countless dishes, I thank my parents, Carol and Russell Cunningham and Homer and Shirley Dedeaux, as well as three masters of fine cuisine, my brothers Devin, David, and Dark Dedeaux. I also thank the finest cook in the world, my grandmother Hilda Warfield.

Finally, my abundant love to the people of the Caribbean and those dear friends who were always there for me: Sherry and Phaedra Delamarter, Mary Morris, Steve and Cleves Weber, Imogen Price, Andrew Mayeux, Colleen and Randy LaGraize, Judy and Al Maeda, Chomper, Bone Pickin Haggaman, Martha Walker Clark Peabody III, Barry and Susan Secular, Lloyd Mailander, and the entire staff and crew of Sugar Reef Restaurant.